PEOPLEISM
A NEW ECONOMIC DAWN

ASHFAQ SYED

INDIA • SINGAPORE • MALAYSIA

ISBN 979-8-89632-835-3

Dedicated to my mother, whose resilience, compassion, and composure have been a constant source of inspiration throughout my life.

CONTENTS

PREFACE

Imagine a world where technology does not replace us—it empowers us. A world where cutting-edge AI technology amplifies human potential, enabling compassionate, human-centered services to thrive. A world where public infrastructure belongs to its citizens, where natural resources generate wealth to build essential systems for everyone, and where the economy is grounded in fairness, opportunity, and shared prosperity.

This is the vision of Peopleism – a bold and transformative economic system designed to meet the challenges of our time. It is a system that measures success not by profits alone but by how it uplifts individuals, strengthens communities, and creates a society where no one is left behind.

In my first book, Everything People: A New Economic System for Our Future, I laid the foundation for a people-centric economy, critiquing the flaws of capitalism and socialism while presenting a vision for collaboration, equity, and shared prosperity. That book was about why we need a new system. Now, in *Peopleism: A New Economic Dawn*, I build on that foundation to explore how we can transition to this new system, addressing the pressing challenges of AI and automation.

For decades, capitalism and socialism have shaped societies, each driving progress in distinct ways, but not without significant costs. Capitalism has concentrated wealth and power in the hands of a few, leaving millions behind. Socialism, with its focus on collective welfare, social progress, universal healthcare, education, and workers' rights, has often been undermined by inefficiency and over-centralized government control. Today, as AI and automation threaten to break the traditional link between work and financial stability, the gap between the privileged few and the struggling majority continues to widen.

We need a new path forward – a system that balances innovation with equity and replaces destructive competition with meaningful collaboration. That system is Peopleism.

At its core, Peopleism puts people—not profits—at the heart of the economy. It envisions a world where technology empowers workers and communities rather than enriching only a privileged few. By decoupling income from traditional jobs, Peopleism ensures financial security for all, redistributes technology-driven wealth equitably, and fosters a more inclusive and sustainable society.

This moment is pivotal, especially for IT professionals. We have built the technological revolutions of the past—from mainframes to mobile. Yet, as AI advances, we risk being sidelined unless we reclaim ownership of the systems we created. Over decades, our work has generated trillions of dollars for corporations and the top 1%. Now, it is time to channel that ingenuity toward empowering ourselves and the 99%.

Here is the reality: the global workforce earns only 20% of the wealth generated worldwide, while an additional 60%—created by technology and infrastructure—most of it goes to the top 1%. That wealth belongs to all of us. By collaborating and taking ownership of technology-driven income, we can decouple earnings from labor, reduce work hours, and ensure financial stability for everyone.

This book brings the vision of Peopleism to life through the conversations of Atif, a technologist, and Sarah, an economist. Atif sees AI and automation as tools capable of generating extraordinary wealth and revolutionizing industries but is worried by the concentration of that technology and wealth in the hands of a few. Sarah critically examines economic systems, questioning why rapid progress often leaves so many behind. She dreams of reimagining the economy to create a society that is inclusive, equitable, and just. Through their debates and collaboration, the framework of Peopleism emerges—a transformative model where technology serves humanity, empowers communities, and redistributes wealth to foster shared prosperity.

Through the seven pillars of Peopleism, this book outlines actionable steps to transform the economy. It emphasizes the role of youth, IT professionals, and knowledge workers as catalysts for this transformation. None of us can afford to be bystanders; we must organize and take control of our shared future.

While Peopleism's principles are universal, this book uses India as a case study. With its vast natural resources, diverse population, and the world's largest youth demographic, India is uniquely positioned to lead this movement. Its dynamic and innovative young generation can show the world how progress can benefit everyone—not just a privileged few.

At its heart, Peopleism is about rewriting the rules of the economy. It is about creating a system where progress uplifts everyone—a world where no one is left behind. This is not just a vision for today but a roadmap for the future.

I hope this book inspires you to dream boldly, act decisively, and join this movement. Together, we can create an economy that truly serves everyone – a future where progress empowers us all.

Welcome to the future. Welcome to Peopleism.

—Ashfaq

Chapter 1

THE AGE OF DISRUPTION

In the not-so-distant future, the world found itself on the brink of monumental change. What had begun as a steady march of technological advancement in the late 20th century had exploded into a wildfire of innovation by the mid-21st century. What once promised economic growth had become an unstoppable force, consuming industries at a breathtaking pace. Information Technology (IT), which had started as a tool to assist humans, had evolved into the engine powering the global economy. Artificial Intelligence (AI), initially confined to routine tasks, now led entire corporations—making decisions, shaping policies, and transforming sectors once thought untouchable by technological disruption.

The effects of this transformation were felt everywhere. Factories, once teeming with human labor, now hummed with the quiet precision of automation. Machines executed tasks with mechanical efficiency, leaving no room for human error. Algorithms dictated billion-dollar investment strategies faster and more accurately than any human financier could. Even hospitals, long dependent on the expertise of doctors and nurses, were now guided by AI systems diagnosing and treating patients faster—and often more effectively—than any human could.

At first glance, it seemed as though the long-promised benefits of technology had finally arrived. Productivity soared, and corporations amassed unprecedented profits. To the casual observer, it appeared to be the culmination of progress: technology had freed humanity from the drudgery of work, and innovation had led to unimaginable prosperity. But beneath this glittering surface, a storm was brewing.

The Personal Cost of Progress

For seasoned IT professionals like Atif, the wave of technological progress was not just theoretical—it was personal. With over three decades of experience, Atif had built his career on innovation, problem-solving, and leadership. He had been at the forefront of the technological revolution, overseeing projects that automated systems, saved companies millions, and streamlined operations. But now, the very systems he had once championed were threatening to make him obsolete.

Years earlier, Atif had led a project to automate the invoicing system of an oil company. The new system saved the company hundreds of hours each month, eliminating the need for an entire invoicing department. Atif had been proud of his work, justifying it as progress. But decades later, he found that the relentless march of automation had made his own career vulnerable. The AI systems he had once seen as tools for human empowerment were now coding, debugging, and optimizing software faster than any human ever could.

As a project manager, Atif had overseen the development of an Enterprise Resource Planning (ERP) system that initially provided jobs for thousands of developers. But as corporate greed crept in, the company was sold and resold to larger, more profit-driven entities. With each acquisition, jobs were cut, and the workforce dwindled from 2,000 employees to just 200. Now, the company was upgrading to an AI-integrated platform, which would slash jobs even further.

Atif was responsible for overseeing this transition, fully aware that it would lead to more layoffs. The faces of his colleagues—people with families, mortgages, and dreams—haunted him. They had once found security and identity in their work, but that security was evaporating.

For Atif, it was not just about losing jobs—it was about losing purpose. Work was not just a paycheck; it was identity, community, and meaning. Without it, people were left adrift in a world that no longer seemed to need them. The younger generation, entering a job market dominated by AI, faced even bleaker prospects. The jobs they had trained for no longer existed. Many were left with gig work or no work at all, teetering on the edge of hopelessness.

One afternoon, over coffee in a café where drones buzzed overhead delivering packages and robots brewed coffee with precision, Atif vented to his friend Sarah. "I've worked my entire life, and now what?"

A System Rigged for Inequality

Sarah, an economist who had spent years studying the economic impacts of capitalism and AI, was deeply aware of how technology was widening the wealth gap. She looked up from her notes and replied thoughtfully, "It is not just you, Atif. It is the entire system. We have handed control of IT, AI, and automation to a handful of corporations. They hoard the wealth these technologies generate, while the rest of us scramble for the leftovers."

Atif nodded. The promise of technology had been hijacked. AI and automation had created unimaginable wealth for a few but left millions feeling irrelevant. Without work, without purpose, what was left for humanity?

Sarah pulled out her tablet and showed Atif a report. "Look at this. Last year, 73% of global income went to the top 1%. Only 27% was shared by the remaining 99%. And here's the kicker—60% of the wealth was created by technology, automation, and infrastructure, without the need for capital or labor."

Atif frowned in thought. "What do you mean, 60% created without capital or labor? How are they getting 73% of the income?"

Sarah explained, "The top 1% owns over 85% of the corporations. These corporations produce the goods and services we all use, and they capture almost all of the profits. The bottom 99% mostly earn their income through work—through employment or wages. But with the rise of automation, work is becoming less valuable, and that means the 99% are getting a smaller and smaller slice of the pie."

"So, the profits from technology go straight to the corporations, leaving everyone else to fend for themselves," Atif said, leaning back, taking it all in.

"Exactly," Sarah replied grimly. "We have a system where wealth is increasingly created by technology but only benefits a small fraction of people."

Reimagining Ownership in the AI Era

Atif's mind raced. If current trends continue, more AI would mean even less wealth for ordinary people. "Let's say AI takes on more roles and creates 50% of our economy's wealth—it also means that half of the work is eliminated, with 10% from infrastructure. That is 60% of wealth that could potentially be owned and managed by the people."

Sarah was skeptical. "I understand the infrastructure; it's mostly public assets that could return to public ownership with the right policies. But how do we reclaim technology already owned by private corporations?"

Atif's face lit up with an idea. "What if we could develop new AI-driven platforms ourselves? Imagine if IT professionals as an organization created AI systems owned by the people. We wouldn't need to rely on corporations."

AI: The Great Equalizer

Sarah's eyes widened. "Are you saying that people—through AI—could create an entirely new economy?"

Atif nodded, his excitement growing. "Yes! AI is a whole new level of technology. It is not just another app or tool that solves one small problem—it is the start of a complete system that can be built from scratch. We are not just talking about single-use apps like rideshare or delivery; AI has the power to transform entire sectors, creating solutions that cover every aspect of an industry."

"Here's how it works," he continued. "An AI platform, or AI infrastructure, would provide the tools for developing specialized AI 'agents'—think of them as intelligent assistants—designed for different sectors. Now, instead of corporations controlling this infrastructure, imagine if *people* owned it. IT professionals and experts in each field could work together, using this shared AI infrastructure to develop agents for every major industry: transportation, healthcare, finance, and beyond."

"Take transportation as an example. Imagine a single AI commuter assistant that seamlessly handles ridesharing, public transit, and carpooling—all without needing separate apps. IT professionals could create platforms like this one, industry by industry, freeing us from corporate control. And because these services would be offered at a fraction of what corporations charge, the savings would go back to the customer support teams, workers, and professionals in each field—everyone would benefit."

Sarah was in awe. "This would completely reshape industries and finally give people a fair share of the wealth."

Atif continued, "When AI is developed by professionals with the goal of easing the burden on workers and distributing its benefits to everyone, the potential for a fairer, more humane society emerges. Rather than concentrating power and wealth in the hands of a few corporations, such an approach can ensure that AI serves the common good. It could reduce job stress, promote better work-life balance, and create new opportunities for economic participation. Moreover, it could decouple income from labor and foster a system where technology is harnessed for societal benefit rather than corporate profit. In this vision, AI becomes a tool for human empowerment, creating a future where work is more meaningful, equitable, and enjoyable for all."

"But if large corporations control this technology," Atif continued, "we face significant risks. They could manipulate public opinion, amass unchecked power, and control wealth on an unprecedented scale, eroding privacy and social stability. Without greater accountability and transparency, these technologies will continue to exacerbate inequality and undermine the democratic and social fabric of society."

Sarah's voice was urgent. "Then we must act. We need to organize and own this technology ourselves."

Peopleism: A New Economic Vision

Sarah sat back, her mind racing with possibilities. "So, you're suggesting that people could own and manage AI, automation, and infrastructure instead of corporations?"

Atif nodded. "That's exactly what I'm saying. Today, corporate overhead—technology, management, customer service—consumes around 40% of revenue. But we could radically change the economy if professionals provided these services through sector-specific cooperative companies at just 20% of the cost. The result would be a system where workers are shareholders, receiving dividends and wages, leading to a livable income, and everyone in the workforce gets income. No more unemployment and underemployment."

Sarah leaned forward, her eyes lighting up. "And it is not just that—think about banks and insurance companies. They are making money off *our* money, and our money is not safe with private corporations that only look at profits for themselves. What if we, the consumers, actually owned them? Imagine banks and insurance companies run by professionals using technology, focused entirely on benefiting their members rather than squeezing out profits."

Atif grinned, nodding. "Exactly! We already have credit unions and cooperative banks, but they are not widespread. Imagine if these institutions were managed professionally and equipped with cutting-edge technology and excellent customer service. They could offer even greater benefits and generate income that goes straight back to the people. It's time for a new economic system—one designed to serve people, not just pad corporate profits."

The Birth of a Movement

For weeks, Sarah had been sketching out this new economic system—one that could rise from the ashes of capitalism and socialism. The new system was an idea born from the failures of the old systems, designed to address the cracks in the foundation that were growing wider every day. She called it Peopleism or People's economy.

What started as an idea was now growing into a movement. Peopleism was an economic vision where the people owned technology, automation, and infrastructure and run by their own communities. No more unemployment, exploitation, or poverty—a fairer future was finally within reach.

* * *

Chapter 2

TRANSITION TO NEW ECONOMIC SYSTEM

The emergence of Peopleism was not a sudden event. It was born out of necessity—a response to the deep flaws in both capitalism and socialism. These systems, which had shaped the global economy for centuries, were no longer equipped to address the realities of the 21st century, particularly with the rise of artificial intelligence (AI) and automation. As Sarah reflected on the potential of Peopleism, she knew that to embrace a new path, they had to understand why the old systems had failed.

Capitalism: Innovation at a Cost

For generations, capitalism was celebrated as the engine of progress. It drove industries to innovate, develop new technologies, and maximize profits. Over time, it lifted millions out of poverty and brought about technological breakthroughs that changed the world. But by the beginning of the 21st century, capitalism had shifted. It no longer served as a driver of broad prosperity; instead, it concentrated wealth and power in the hands of a few.

"Look at tech giants like Amazon, Microsoft, Google, and Apple," Sarah would often say to Atif. "They do not just compete—they dominate entire industries, manipulating, automating to reduce manpower, controlling data, infrastructure, and now eliminating even the very employees who built these companies. With AI, they are not just optimizing work; they are eliminating it."

Atif, who had seen these changes up close during his career in IT, nodded in agreement. "These corporations use technology to consolidate power. They have cut jobs, leaving people with fewer options and less security. When they are making billions in revenue."

The problem, Sarah explained, was that capitalism rewarded those who owned the means of production, not those who did the actual work. "Wealth is not flowing to the people who work hard. It is flowing to those who control the technology," she said. "Last year alone, 73% of global income went to the top 1%."

The promise of capitalism—success through hard work—was collapsing under the weight of AI and automation. With machines taking over human labor, wealth was concentrated in the hands of those who owned the platforms, leaving workers struggling to find a place in the economy.

Socialism: Equality at the Cost of Innovation

While capitalism created inequality, socialism aimed to distribute wealth more equally by placing the means of production in the hands of the state and workers. Socialism's goal was to eliminate poverty by ensuring everyone had access to essentials like housing, healthcare, and education.

However, socialism had its own limitations, as Sarah pointed out. "The issue with socialism is that while it promotes equality, it often sacrifices innovation. Government-run industries tend to resist technological advancements because they disrupt the status quo."

Atif, having observed the decline of various state-run industries, added, "In these systems, there's little motivation to improve. People get paid regardless of productivity, so innovation stalls. And in today's fast-paced world, that stagnation can be deadly."

Socialism avoided the extreme wealth inequality seen in capitalism, but it failed to generate the growth needed to keep up with a modern, technology-driven society. This lack of competitiveness and reluctance to embrace innovation left socialism unable to adapt to the pace of change brought about by AI and automation.

The Need for a New System

As Sarah and Atif debated the merits and flaws of capitalism and socialism, they found themselves at a crossroads. Capitalism fostered innovation but entrenched vast inequality. Socialism, on the other hand, prioritized equality but often came at the cost of growth and innovation. They agreed: neither system could fully address the challenges of the 21st century. What the world needed was a new economic paradigm—one that combined the strengths of both systems while avoiding their weaknesses. Thus, the foundation of **Peopleism** was born.

"Peopleism," Sarah explained, "is about shared ownership. Instead of allowing corporations or governments to control the wealth created by technology, that wealth would belong to the people who build and sustain it."

Atif leaned in, energized. "Especially now, with AI being such a transformative technology. It does not rely on prior systems, so this is the perfect time for us—IT professionals—to develop it and claim ownership."

"Exactly," Sarah nodded. "Under Peopleism, profits from AI, automation, and infrastructure would not flow exclusively to a handful of corporate owners. They would be shared among the workers and communities that depend on these systems. Cooperative company ownership is the cornerstone. Professionals would manage industries, but wealth would be distributed fairly."

Atif's eyes lit up with curiosity. "That sounds like a real solution – but it would require completely rethinking our economic structure."

"Absolutely," Sarah replied, painting a vivid picture of Peopleism in action. "Imagine this: the people who create and maintain technology actually own part of it. IT professionals would not just get salaries—they would earn royalties and dividends from the tech they create. Each type of service provider like technology provider, customer service management service, or sector-specific service providers will have a role to play. A share of the technology profits would go to the innovators, while the rest would benefit service providers and the wider community. It is a system where everyone shares in the prosperity."

Atif nodded thoughtfully. "So, it's about shared ownership. People don't just control technology and infrastructure – they share the wealth it generates."

Sarah smiled. "Exactly. Peopleism combines innovation with fairness. The more efficient and productive our systems become, the more everyone benefits. Take jobs as an example. Today, if AI improves productivity by 50%, that often means 50% of jobs disappear. But in Peopleism, those productivity gains would be shared. Instead of half the workforce losing jobs, everyone would work 50% fewer hours while maintaining—or even increasing—their income. AI would handle repetitive tasks, freeing people for creativity, leisure, and personal growth."

She continued, her tone growing urgent. "The imbalance today is staggering. The top 1% control 73% of income—not because they work harder, but because they own the technology and infrastructure driving wealth creation. Here is the breakdown:

- **20% of wealth** goes to people as wages for their labor.

- **20%** rewards capital investments.

- The remaining **60%**, created by technology and infrastructure, overwhelmingly benefits the top 1%—they take **53%**, leaving just **7%** for everyone else."

Atif looked stunned. "So, this isn't just about fairness – it's about reclaiming what's rightfully ours."

Sarah nodded. "Exactly. That 60% is the gap we need to bridge. Through the pillars of Peopleism, we can shift the balance. Every step—whether it is cooperative ownership, friendly customer service, publicly managed AI, or infrastructure, customer-owned banks and insurance—tilts the scales toward people. Once all the pillars are in place, the balance will finally favor the people."

Under Peopleism, technology would no longer serve as a profit engine for corporations – it would become a tool to uplift entire communities. Wealth would not be hoarded by the privileged few but shared equitably. Publicly owned technology, physical infrastructure, and energy systems would generate wealth that is reinvested in education, healthcare, and universal basic income.

"This is more than an economic shift," Sarah concluded. "It's a movement to spread prosperity, empowering everyone—not just the elite—to thrive in the modern world."

The Seven Pillars of Peopleism: A Blueprint for a New Economic Era

To bring Peopleism to life, Sarah and Atif realized it needed more than ideals; it required a robust framework—a vision that would inspire and guide action. Together, they crafted the **Seven Pillars of Peopleism**, a transformative foundation for an economy that puts people at its heart.

1. *Organizing Society by Networks*

Peopleism reimagines how society interacts with the economy by organizing it into **four interconnected networks**:

- **Workers**: Grouped by their sectors, ensuring fair representation and participation in economic benefits.

- **Residents**: Strengthening local communities to address local challenges and foster collaboration.

- **Consumers**: Advocating for fair markets, ethical production, quality products and services at lower prices, and sustainable consumption.

- **Citizens**: Protecting democracy by empowering everyone to shape governance and policy.

These networks ensure that everyone has a voice and a stake in the system, turning fragmented individuals into a united force for change.

2. *Empowering IT Professionals to Develop and Own AI*

In a world reshaped by AI and technology, Peopleism redefines the role of IT professionals, ensuring they are empowered as creators and co-owners of the systems they develop. Instead of monopolizing the entire system, their focus is on designing, managing, and maintaining the technology while respective service providers handle its implementation and operation. For their contributions, IT professionals receive income for their services and royalties for their ownership.

Key elements of this pillar include:

- **Global IT Professionals Leading Innovation:** IT professionals develop AI technologies through collaborative network startups, driving innovation tailored to societal needs.

- **Formation of Cooperative Companies:** In each country, IT professionals establish cooperative companies to maintain and implement these technologies locally.

- **Equitable Revenue Distribution:** Rather than profits being concentrated in a few corporations, revenue is fairly distributed. IT professionals earn a significant portion, while sector-specific workers and consumers benefit from reduced prices and improved access to goods and services.

This model ensures that technology becomes a tool for empowerment, driving innovation while fostering equity and inclusivity. By aligning technology with the principles of Peopleism, this pillar transforms AI from a force of exploitation to a source of shared prosperity.

3. *Customer Service and Management Cooperatives*

In Peopleism, the essential functions of customer service and management for sector-specific companies will be handled by **worker-owned cooperative company of customer service and management professionals.** These cooperative companies will use the AI tools and provide friendly and compassionate support services for the entire economy. It represents a transformative approach to delivering services, ensuring both quality and sustainability.

- **Professionally Managed Operations:** These cooperatives will leverage advanced IT and AI tools to boost efficiency, streamline processes, and enhance productivity.

- **High-Quality Service Delivery:** Acting on behalf of organizations and sector-specific companies, they will ensure top-tier services are consistently delivered to consumers.

By equipping workers with cutting-edge technology and fostering professional management practices, these cooperatives create a model for delivering ethical, high-quality, and sustainable products and services. This approach not only empowers workers but also guarantees consumers receive superior care and value, making the economy work for everyone.

4. *Sector-Specific Worker-Owned Companies*

Imagine industries run by the workers who power them. In Peopleism, every industry would have:

- **Worker-owned cooperative companies**, replacing fragmented and inefficient businesses.

- The cooperative company would get all the AI and automation tools required for that sector to provide efficient and quality products and services.

- Professional management and customer service cooperatives to ensure smooth operations.

- Profits distributed as **dividends** to worker-owners, alongside fair wages for their labor.

This model creates a more equitable economy where everyone in the workforce is a participant, not a spectator, ensuring service providers get more than a livable income, working less and with economic inclusion.

5. *Consumer-Owned Banks and Insurance Companies*

Financial institutions like banks and insurance providers play a vital role in managing people's money. However, when controlled by private corporations, they can expose the public to significant risks, including the loss of financial security and well-being. Under Peopleism, these institutions would operate on a transformative model:

- **Collective Ownership:** Banks and insurance companies would be collectively owned by their customers, ensuring that the primary focus is on serving the people's needs rather than corporate interests.

- **Advanced Technology and Professional Management:** Leveraging cutting-edge IT and AI technology, along with skilled management and customer service professionals, these institutions would operate with high efficiency, security, and reliability.

- **Profit Redistribution:** Instead of profits being funneled to private shareholders, they would be distributed back to the members, aligning the institution's goals with the collective well-being of its customers.

This approach fosters a financial system that is safe, transparent, and centered on serving society. By prioritizing collective benefit over profit maximization, it creates institutions that truly work for the people.

6. *Publicly Owned Infrastructure: The Backbone of Prosperity*

Infrastructure is the lifeline of any economy, and in Peopleism, it takes on a transformative role:

- **Collective Ownership:** Critical systems such as roads, warehouses, schools and colleges, hospitals and other healthcare facilities, power grids, renewable energy facilities, cloud computing, and AI platforms would be owned by the public, managed through a sovereign fund or an independent asset management company. This ensures accountability and transparency, keeping these essential resources free from exploitation.

- **Independence from Corruption and Profiteering:** Unlike private corporations or government-controlled entities, which often prioritize profit or are prone to corruption, these publicly owned assets would be managed by an **independent, people owned organization** dedicated solely to societal benefit.

- **Reinvestment for the Public Good:** The wealth generated by these resources would be reinvested in society, funding critical services such as universal healthcare, education, and guaranteed income programs, creating a ripple effect of prosperity.

By keeping infrastructure in public hands, Peopleism establishes a sustainable and equitable foundation for economic growth, ensuring that the benefits of these essential systems flow directly to the people.

7. *Natural Resources for the People: A Shared Legacy*

Natural resources are the collective wealth of everyone—not a privilege for a select few. In Peopleism, this principle is the foundation for fairness and sustainability:

- Managed in the Public Interest: Natural resources would be responsibly managed to prioritize the long-term good of society. Recognizing their finite nature, revenues generated from these resources would be strategically invested in building sustainable infrastructure—spanning technology, physical infrastructure, and renewable energy sectors.

- Stable Income for All: Once sustainable infrastructure is in place, the revenues and rents generated from these assets would fund a guaranteed income for all citizens. This reflects the shared ownership of the nation's natural wealth, ensuring economic stability and equity for everyone.

By transforming natural wealth into a collective asset for societal progress, this approach prevents private profiteering and creates a sustainable, inclusive economy. Through Peopleism, natural resources become a shared legacy, converted into critical and essential infrastructure, safeguarded for the prosperity of present and future generations.

The Vision of Peopleism These seven pillars are not just ideas—they are a roadmap for an economic revolution. By organizing society into networks, empowering workers and consumers, and ensuring shared ownership of resources, Peopleism offers a bold alternative to the inequalities of capitalism and the inefficiencies of socialism. It is a system where everyone has a stake and where the economy truly works for the people.

From Crisis to Opportunity

As their discussion wrapped up, Sarah and Atif reflected on the journey they had taken. Capitalism and socialism had both reached their limits, unable to cope with the realities of an AI-driven, technologically advanced world. But Peopleism offered a new path – a system that combined the best of both worlds while avoiding their pitfalls.

"This is the future," Sarah said confidently. "Peopleism is about reclaiming control over our lives and economies. It's about using technology not just for profit, but for the common good."

Atif smiled. "It's about time."

The age of Peopleism was no longer just a concept; it was becoming a movement ready to reshape the world.

* * *

Chapter 3

REDEFINING COMMUNITY AND ORGANIZING

Sarah gazed out of the window of her study, watching autumn leaves swirl in the breeze, their movement mirroring the profound changes Peopleism promised. Her career had been built on fighting for workers' rights, organizing unions, and advocating for fairness in a capitalist world. Those battles were hard-won, yet now she sensed something even bigger was within reach—a future where people connected and organized in ways that could transform society.

She realized that the old structures, like unions and professional associations, were focused on work. But in a world where income was not linked to labor, those forms of organizing would be obsolete. People engaged with the economy not just as workers; they were also consumers, community members, and citizens. To create a cohesive community, she thought, they would need new types of organizations based on how they truly interacted with society.

Just then, Atif knocked and stepped inside, sensing her excitement. "Sarah, you look like you're onto something big," he said, sitting across from her, curiosity in his eyes.

Sarah smiled, appreciating his intuition. "I've been thinking about how Peopleism changes everything—especially how we organize ourselves.

Traditional unions, trade associations, employee associations—those were essential when jobs and income were central to survival. But in a world where income isn't solely tied to labor, those old models don't work anymore."

Atif nodded thoughtfully. "With Peopleism, the old rules don't apply. But we'll still need ways for people to connect and support one another, right?"

"Exactly," Sarah replied. "But the structure will align with Peopleist values—shared ownership, universal participation, and empowerment. I am imagining four new networks based on how we engage with the economy: as workers, residents, consumers, and citizens. Each one would allow people to connect, contribute, and thrive in their own ways."

Atif leaned forward, intrigued. "Four networks? That sounds revolutionary. Tell me more."

1. Occupation-Based Networks: Reimagining Professional Life

Sarah's face lit up as she began. "The occupation-based networks will go beyond traditional unions. They will not just represent workers' interests; they will support everyone in a sector, whether employed, between jobs, or retired. These networks will provide training, career support, and connect people with industry advancements throughout their lives."

Atif thought of Rohan, a friend who had lost his job to automation. "Rohan would have loved that. When his engineering job was automated, he felt completely abandoned."

'In Peopleism, Rohan would not have been left out,' Sarah said. 'His network would keep him updated on industry trends, help him reskill, and provide income as a shareholder in his sector's wealth. These networks ensure everyone benefits from automation and AI—not just those actively working.'

Atif raised an eyebrow, impressed. "So, even if a job gets automated, people remain connected to their industry's wealth?"

"Precisely," Sarah replied. "Even if a machine takes over your role, you still receive dividends from automation and technology used to produce products or services delivered. These networks will offer opportunities, skill-building, and ensure people can grow and adapt."

Atif looked amazed. "That is a profound shift. People will not fear automation – they will see it as a chance to evolve."

2. Resident-Based Networks: Rebuilding Local Communities

Sarah leaned forward. "The second network is resident-based networks, which will redefine how people engage with their communities. Today, neighborhood associations are often powerless. In a Peopleist society, everyone would belong to a professionally managed network based on where they live, with a real say in local matters."

Atif thought of Maya, a friend who had struggled to get local issues addressed. "Maya spent years trying to fix the potholes on her street but couldn't get any help."

"In a resident-based network, she would have had real support," Sarah said. "These networks would not just address issues—they would handle local services like utilities, healthcare access, and education. It's a system that empowers people to actively improve their community."

Atif nodded. "And it is more than services. It is about building connections."

"Yes," Sarah agreed. "These networks would be there during crises, fostering mutual support systems. People would face challenges together rather than alone."

3. Consumer-Based Networks: Empowering Buyers

Sarah's eyes lit up again. "The third network is consumer-based. Today, consumers are isolated and often at the mercy of corporations. In a Peopleist society, they'll be organized, empowered to negotiate for better prices, and protected by dedicated support teams."

Atif laughed. "So, no more endless hours on hold with customer service?"

"Exactly! Think about Afrin, who spends hours comparing prices just to save on groceries. In a consumer-based network, her group would negotiate directly with suppliers to get the best deals for everyone, and if she faced an issue, her network's support team would be there to help."

Atif grinned. "That's a huge shift. Instead of helpless buyers, people will have real power in the marketplace."

4. Citizen-Based Networks: Redefining Democracy

Finally, Sarah said, "The fourth network is citizen-based, transforming how we participate in democracy. Today, people vote every few years but feel disconnected from real decision-making. Citizen-based networks will change that."

Atif leaned in, intrigued. "How so?"

"These networks will allow for continuous, participatory governance," Sarah explained. "People will have a say in policies, resource allocation, and public services year-round, not just during election season. Imagine people voting on issues that impact their lives in real-time, using transparent, community-driven platforms."

She thought of Jay, an environmental activist frustrated by corporate lobbyists. "In Peopleism, Jay's network would let him directly contribute to policy discussions and hold officials accountable. It's real democracy, not just symbolic voting."

Atif's eyes widened. "So, people can actively shape their communities and government?"

"Yes," Sarah said. "And it is not just about governance. Public resources—healthcare, infrastructure, education—will be collectively owned. Profits will be reinvested into society, ensuring everyone benefits."

The Future of Organizing

Sarah paused, letting the full vision settle in. "Atif, these networks will change everything. It is about moving from survival to thriving. Peopleism decouples income from labor but also provides support in every area of life—through work, community, consumer choices, and civic participation."

Atif smiled, understanding the depth of her vision. "It's a complete reimagining of society—a world where people are empowered, connected, and supported, no matter what."

Sarah nodded; her eyes filled with hope. "Yes, that's exactly it. Peopleism is not just about wealth. It is about giving everyone a stake in society, a voice in their future, and ensuring no one is left behind."

✳ ✳ ✳

Chapter 4

RECLAIMING TECHNOLOGY FOR PEOPLE

Peopleism emerged at a pivotal moment when technology was transforming every corner of society. Information Technology (IT) had become the backbone of industries ranging from banking and healthcare to agriculture and entertainment. Yet, a troubling reality had come into sharp focus: while IT professionals built the systems powering this transformation, the wealth and control flowed to a handful of massive corporations.

As Artificial Intelligence (AI) advanced at lightning speed, Sarah and Atif, the architects of Peopleism, saw an unprecedented opportunity. They believed that if IT professionals could not only build but also own the AI infrastructure, the benefits would ripple out to professionals, local economies, and the public good.

Atif had spent nearly 30 years navigating the IT landscape, witnessing its power to revolutionize industries. His career was a front-row seat to technological milestones. He recalled the early days when banks digitized their services, freeing customers from long queues and offering 24/7 access through sleek apps. Healthcare systems became more efficient, travel was simplified, and education became more accessible—all thanks to IT innovation. Industries once bogged down by inefficiencies were now thriving in a digital-first world.

But Atif also saw a darker side to this transformation. Despite IT driving massive profitability for businesses, the professionals behind the breakthroughs were often left behind. Corporations reaped the rewards, while the engineers and developers who created the wealth remained mere cogs in the machine.

"We built billion-dollar empires," Atif often said, "but we don't have anything to show for it."

Sarah echoed his frustration with hard data. "The IT sector already generates 40% of the world's wealth, but less than 5% of that reaches the people creating the technology. With AI, it is expected to exceed 50%. If we don't change the system, those profits will go straight to Big Tech shareholders."

Atif nodded grimly. "AI should be a tool for everyone, not just another asset for corporations to extract rent from. This is our chance to make AI work for all of us."

The Shift to AI: Large Language Models and a Unified Vision

The emergence of large language models (LLMs) like ChatGPT marked a significant turning point in the world of technology. These advanced AI systems had the capacity to understand natural language, generate ideas, write code, and build complex systems with unprecedented efficiency. For Atif, the potential of LLMs was a revelation.

"Sarah," he said with urgency, "we no longer need massive budgets or reliance on corporate giants to create groundbreaking technology. With LLMs, a robust AI infrastructure, and high-quality data, we have the tools to build these platforms ourselves—if we work together."

He paused to gather his thoughts, then continued, "For years, corporations have been telling IT professionals to 'become entrepreneurs'— to start their own companies. But what happens? Thousands of small startups emerge, each trying to solve a tiny part of a much larger problem. Most of them fail within the first year, wasting valuable resources and energy. Instead of collaborating, they end up competing, duplicating efforts, and achieving very little. What we need is a unified approach—a global network where IT professionals join forces to solve the big problems in every sector, on a global scale."

Sarah's expression lit up as the concept clicked. "Imagine this," she said, her voice rising with excitement, "a global structure that connects IT professionals to work collectively, solving problems in agriculture, healthcare, education, and beyond. We could organize globally, leveraging shared expertise and resources while still adapting solutions to fit the unique needs of each country. In this system, IT professionals would not just be workers—they would be owners. They'd share in the wealth they create and ensure the benefits extend to the service providers and communities who use the technology."

Atif nodded, encouraged by her enthusiasm. "Exactly. By collaborating instead of competing, we can build sector-wide solutions that are scalable, efficient, and inclusive. IT professionals would finally have the chance to reclaim ownership of the systems they create, while simultaneously driving global progress. This is not just about solving problems—it is about reshaping how technology serves humanity."

Together, they envisioned a revolutionary system where IT professionals worldwide worked as a cohesive network to build and own the future of IT and AI. This was not just an idea—it was the foundation of Peopleism, where technology's wealth would no longer be concentrated in the hands of corporations but shared with those who built it and the communities it served.

Part 1: GITProNet—The Global IT Professionals Network

To bring their vision to life, Sarah and Atif knew they needed a global platform connecting IT professionals, network startups, global vendor network, and local IT service companies. They envisioned **GITProNet— the Global IT Professionals Network**—a collaborative platform designed to unite and empower IT professionals worldwide. GITProNet would serve as a hub for tools, training, resources, and community.

"GITProNet would be like a worldwide association for IT professionals," Sarah explained. "Here, they can access tools, receive training, and collaborate on meaningful projects. Everyone would have a place to share ideas and work together."

Atif added, "And it is more than just technology. GITProNet would provide career support, infrastructure, and ongoing education. It would be a global community that's got your back, whether you're in India, Brazil, or the US."

How GITProNet Functions:

- **Resource Hub**: GITProNet would provide access to shared tools, code libraries, and technical assistance to speed up development across network startups.

- **Collaborative Projects**: IT professionals could team up across borders, drawing insights from different markets and building solutions tailored to local needs.

- **Government Collaboration**: Recognizing the need for local infrastructure, GITProNet would work with governments to implement technology infrastructure and drive innovation.

Sarah imagined the impact. "This network gives IT professionals real power. Instead of being workers within a system, they can shape IT and AI globally."

Part 2: Technology Vendor Network—Streamlining Access and Support

The second part of their ecosystem would be the **Technology Vendor Network**, designed to streamline the supply of technology resources. Today, technology vendors sell directly as software-as-a-service (SaaS) or provide products directly to consumers in various countries. But Sarah and Atif proposed a new model where all technology requirements would flow through a local IT services company owned by IT professionals of that country, ensuring fair pricing and local support for products and services. The tech developed by network startups will also be routed through this network. As the new tech is developed by the IT professionals' owned network startup, it will replace the corporate-owned technology.

"The vendor network would ensure that every country has access to the necessary technology at fair prices," Atif explained. "Local IT service companies could manage support and distribution, giving consumers access to quality tech products and services at reasonable prices."

By coordinating with local vendors, the network would optimize the supply chain, allowing consumers to receive reliable service and the IT professionals who manage them to earn fair, transparent income.

Part 3: Network Startups—Building Sector-Specific AI Solutions

The heart of the Peopleist ecosystem would be **Network Startups**, sector-specific, IT professional-owned companies focused on solving real needs in healthcare, education, travel, transportation, and more. Unlike traditional startups with a singular profit motive, these network startups would focus on building tailored AI tools for each industry, directly benefiting the creators and meeting local needs.

"Picture this," Atif said, "a healthcare network startup, one for transportation, another for banking. Each startup is owned by IT professionals and professionals in the industry, and they build AI solutions that solve actual problems instead of just maximizing profits. Once the solutions are developed, they are handed over to the local IT services company in each country. The network startups are funded by the IT professionals and related sector professionals."

Sarah could see the advantages immediately. "This way, instead of dozens of companies solving bits of each issue, we would have network startups that address all sector-specific problems. They could pool resources, share insights, and customize AI for each country's needs."

With LLMs accelerating their development, these startups would collaborate with local IT professionals who understand the country's needs. Each startup would receive assistance from GITProNet, gaining access to resources, infrastructure, and expertise while remaining locally managed.

How It Works:

- **Professional Ownership**: Network startups are controlled by IT professionals and industry professionals around the world, allowing them to build without pressure from outside investors.

- **Sector-Specific Focus**: Each network startup builds solutions tailored to the industry it serves, responding directly to local needs.

- **Global Connection**: Each startup shares resources, expertise, and insights with other teams globally, creating a cooperative AI ecosystem across borders.

- **Network startup funding:** the network startups are funded by the global IT professionals and related professionals.

Part 4: Cooperative IT Services Companies—Locally Managed, Publicly Accessible Technology

At the core of the Peopleist ecosystem would be **Cooperative IT Services Companies** established in each country. Unlike the startups, these companies would not develop technology. Instead, they would focus on providing services, implementing, and managing technology infrastructure within each sector, making sure services remain accessible to all and tailored to local needs.

"This would be a completely different approach," Sarah said excitedly. "Instead of seeing infrastructure as something to profit from, it is a public resource to serve everyone. Because these cooperatives own the infrastructure, no one can buy or privatize it." Atif extended the conversation to say, "In fact, many countries or states within the country have similar public companies to procure IT solutions from the vendor network. But IT professionals do not benefit from it. These cooperative companies are better."

In these cooperative companies, IT professionals would be shareholders. They would not only work to implement technology across sectors but also earn royalties from the systems they helped build. This model would allow them to bring national services to life, from AI healthcare tools to national transportation systems, without needing private investors.

Key Benefits of Cooperative IT Services Companies:

- **Ownership by IT Professionals**: IT professionals collectively own the cooperative companies, ensuring stable and equitable distribution of income.

- **National Technology Infrastructure**: Professionals maintain, upgrade, and manage each country's technology infrastructure as a public asset.

- **Equitable and Stable Income**: In addition to their work income, IT professionals receive royalties as shareholders of network startups and income from services the company provides.

Atif imagined the long-term impact. "For the first time, IT professionals would be shareholders. Not just working for a paycheck but earning from the systems they help build. And dividends from the IT services provided in their country as shareholders."

How It All Comes Together: A Unified Peopleist AI Ecosystem

With GITProNet, Network Startups, the Technology Vendor Network, and Cooperative IT Services Companies, Sarah and Atif had mapped out a complete ecosystem for IT and AI development and deployment. Each component of the Peopleist AI ecosystem was interconnected, creating a self-sustaining structure that could be adapted to any country, sharing expertise globally while responding to local needs.

To illustrate how this could transform society, Atif shared a familiar example. "Look at the transportation industry. Today, we have Uber, Lyft, Bolt—all providing similar services and raising prices. Drivers and users both pay the price while only the corporation's profit."

Sarah nodded. "But in the Peopleist model, a single AI-powered platform developed by the Network Startup in transportation and managed by the IT services company would coordinate all transportation needs."

They envisioned an AI healthcare system coordinating patient care, from affordable consultations to wellness advice, empowering doctors and ensuring affordability for patients. In education, cooperatively developed

AI could create adaptive learning programs accessible to all, regardless of background or income.

The beauty of the Peopleist ecosystem is its ability to eliminate private companies in essential services. Instead of needing separate platforms and apps for each service, users would engage directly with AI-powered solutions. And since these solutions are owned and managed by IT professionals, the wealth generated would be shared among the professionals who built and maintained it, workers and professionals who use the systems to provide services, and consumers with lower costs.

A People-Driven Revolution in Technology

Sarah and Atif's Peopleist AI ecosystem embodied a revolutionary vision. Technology would no longer be a tool controlled from above but owned by those who create it and does not hoard all the profits. The owners take their income and pass the benefits to the service providers of each sector.

"The power of AI is transformative," Sarah reflected. "But if we can direct it toward public good, it will change everything."

Atif smiled. "And this time, we are not just users or employees. We are owners and creators. With Network Startups, GITProNet, and Cooperative IT Services, we have designed an ecosystem where IT professionals have control."

This Peopleist model redefines the relationship between people and technology. Each component of the ecosystem supports the others, creating an AI-driven world that empowers people rather than exploiting them. It is a world where services are affordable, transparent, and cooperation driven. It is a world built on shared ownership, fair pay, and sustainable growth.

For Sarah and Atif, this was not just a vision; it was a plan, a blueprint for building an AI ecosystem that would transform society and help give the AI technology income to the professionals, service providers, and people. The Peopleist ecosystem was not a distant hope but a tangible path forward—a revolution in technology ownership, ready to empower communities and shape a fairer future.

Sarah's inner economist lit up as she smiled and said, "When IT professionals own and control AI and IT infrastructure, we can add another 10% to the income and wealth of the 99%. Combined with the 20% people already earn through their labor, that is 30% of the wealth in the hands of the majority. It is still 30:70, skewed toward the top 1%, but as each sector of the economy is reclaimed, the balance will shift. Eventually, it will tilt in favor of the people."

❋ ❋ ❋

Chapter 5

CUSTOMER SERVICE AND MANAGEMENT

By the late 20th century, technology and automation had drastically transformed industries, enabling companies to mass-produce goods and expand their services globally. From manufacturing to retail, businesses leveraged these advancements to scale operations and enhance productivity. However, this surge in growth introduced a significant and often overlooked challenge: providing adequate customer support.

In the earlier decades, customer service was personal and responsive. Representatives, whether over the phone or in person, had the authority to resolve issues in favor of the customer. Atif, an IT professional, had lived through this era and witnessed firsthand how customer service declined in quality as businesses expanded and became more reliant on automation. Living in both the U.S. and India during the 1990s, he often compared customer service in the two countries. In the U.S., service was exceptional by his standards, with problems being solved quickly and almost always in favor of the customer. Whether speaking to a representative over the phone or at a front desk, Atif noticed that these employees had real decision-making power. They could resolve issues without constantly needing managerial approval. Even when cases were escalated to managers, the result was almost always in the customer's favor. Every company had a budget of 10% cost associated with customer service.

In Atif's view, the saying "the customer is king" was more than just a slogan in the U.S. during the 90s—it was a reality. Companies took pride in their customer service, and customers expected a certain level of care and attention when they had an issue. But by the early 2000s, this dynamic began to change. Complaints were no longer addressed with the same care, and the power of customer service representatives and managers to assist customers started to fade.

As companies expanded and customer bases grew, they leaned heavily on automation, and Atif soon recognized this shift. He explained to Sarah, "Technology changed everything." He went on to describe how businesses, in an effort to cut costs and scale operations, had begun to implement automated systems to handle customer service interactions. "Software systems had to be programmed with set rules," he said, "and that left no room for the flexibility that once allowed to bend in favor of the customer. As the customer base increased, the 10% cost started to prick the management and that is when the shift to technology and automation started in customer service.

Atif pointed to a simple example: car rentals. "If you rented a midsize car and it was not available, the representative could upgrade you to a full-size car at no extra charge," he said. "Now, with automated systems, the software only allows an upgrade if you pay an additional fee. The personal touch is gone." This rigidity, he explained, became the norm across industries. As these systems grew more sophisticated, customer service representatives lost their power to make decisions. Companies, more interested in cutting costs than in helping customers, started using technology to hide their human employees behind layers of automation.

"When customers called with a problem, they were met with an automated system trying to resolve it using rigid, pre-programmed responses," Atif lamented. "The few persistent ones who held on for an hour or two might eventually reach a human, but most would have their issues resolved against them." Automation had created a barrier between customers and the help they needed, turning what was once a responsive service into a frustrating ordeal.

Sarah, listening intently, was stunned. "How can companies treat their customers like that without losing them?" she asked.

Atif smiled wryly. "When every company starts doing the same thing, people stop expecting good customer service. It is no longer a factor they consider when choosing a company. Poor service becomes the norm, and customers just accept it." Over time, businesses had collectively lowered the bar for customer service, and consumers, in turn, had grown accustomed to it.

Sarah pressed further. "But what about when people buy products or services? Do not they ask questions to make sure they are getting the right thing?"

Atif chuckled. "That is the clever part. These days, everything is bought online or through apps. The responsibility is shifted to the consumer to do their research. If you buy something that does not fit your needs, well, it is your fault for not doing your due diligence. And as for terms and conditions? They are always full of clauses that favor the company, not the customer. But no one reads them. They just sign blindly, agreeing to things that are not in their best interest."

Sarah was incredulous. "How do companies get away with this? Are not there consumer courts and regulations to stop this?"

Atif nodded but explained, "Yes, we have consumer protection laws, but they are easily circumvented. Out of millions of complaints, only a handful ever reach a court, and even when the ruling is in favor of the customer, it is a drop in the bucket for these corporations. They consider it part of the cost of doing business."

The conversation shifted to the future as Sarah asked, "What about AI? Will not it improve customer service?"

Atif's expression darkened. "Not likely. As long as customer service remains in the hands of companies, AI will only make things worse. The AI systems will be programmed to protect the company's interests, not the customers. We are already seeing it. Look around. When was the last time you interacted with a human during a transaction? Just the other day, I flew to Atlanta and did not speak to a single airline employee until I reached the gate. I checked in through a machine, printed my own boarding pass, tagged my luggage, and even scanned my ticket at the gate myself. The only thing I did not do was fly the plane!"

Sarah's frustration was palpable. "So, with AI, not only are there no jobs for people, but customers are also left to fend for themselves. And companies are still charging us extra for 'customer service'? What a disaster! And do not forget, just managing essential services like gas, water, electricity, internet, insurance, banking—each one is a different company. That is easily a dozen companies we deal with just for day-to-day living. Imagine how much time and frustration we spend on this, not to mention the research we have to do. Automation and technology have not made life easier; they have outsourced all the work to us!"

Atif nodded in agreement. "Exactly. It is a scam. In the old days, you had travel agents, insurance agents—people whose job was to do the research and due diligence for you. Now, companies have taken that support away, forcing us to do everything ourselves."

The conversation took a turn toward solutions as Sarah asked, "So, how do we fix this?"

Atif smiled. "We take customer service back. We move the customer service away from the product and service providers. What if there was a cooperative company, owned by the customer service providers themselves, that worked on behalf of consumers? This company could handle the research, represent us, and interact with corporations on our behalf. They would use AI and technology, not to cut corners, but to serve customers more efficiently."

Sarah's eyes lit up. "That is brilliant! But who pays for it? Customers will not want to pay an extra 10% for better service."

Atif shook his head. "The customers will not have to pay. The companies already allocate a portion of their costs for customer service—about 10%. They will just direct that amount to the customer service cooperative company."

Sarah raised an eyebrow. "Why would companies agree to that? They are focused on cutting costs, not adding more."

Atif remained confident. "It will eventually become a bottleneck for them. Besides, they have already added 10% to customer service for their products and services. If consumers demand it, and if it is backed by regulation, they will not have a choice. In fact, it is beneficial for them. They will not have to deal with millions of individual customers. Think of how airports work. When you buy a flight ticket, a portion of that fare goes to airport taxes, security fees, and service fees for things like baggage handling. The airlines pay those fees because they are part of the system. Similarly, customer service fees could be separated at the source and paid directly to a specialized company that is accountable to consumers. This concept could even start with government services."

Sarah nodded, seeing the vision clearly. "And in Peopleism, this cooperative company could be powered by technology and AI to provide high-quality service, with the profits shared among the workers. No more layoffs, no more frustrated customers—just a system that actually works for people."

Atif added, "More than just customer service, this cooperative workforce—educated and well-trained—will be the driving force behind Peopleism. They will help organize other sectors, professionally manage and support sector-based cooperative companies, and ensure that consumers receive the services they need."

Sarah smiled. "This could be transformative. They will use AI and IT developed by the IT services cooperative company to help the entire economy. It will employ 10% of the workforce with technology support; they will work fewer hours, but as real friends of the people and still make living wages. Finally, we have found a support system for the people."

In Atif and Sarah's vision, this customer service model would restore the balance between companies and consumers. It would not only make customer service more effective but also elevate it to a critical part of the economy under Peopleism. Rather than being a cost-cutting measure, customer service would become a key pillar of economic justice, redistributing power from corporations to the people. This cooperative approach could be applied across various industries, creating a new norm where technology serves the people rather than oppressing them.

They believed this would be the future of customer service in Peopleism—where customers are no longer left to fend for themselves and where AI and automation are harnessed to improve lives rather than increase profits at the expense of service. The revolution in customer service could spark a broader transformation across industries, bringing the Peopleism model to life, one cooperative company at a time.

Management support for organizations and cooperatives

Atif emphasized the crucial role of management professionals in making Peopleism a reality. He explained to Sarah, "Management graduates, with their expertise in corporate functions—like human resources, marketing, project supervision, and operations—are essential for the transition to Peopleism. We have customer support covered, but for Peopleism to succeed, sector-specific cooperatives and organizations need professional management to operate effectively and profitably. While the IT sector will provide AI and digital tools, the management professionals will oversee these cooperatives and organizations, ensuring they run efficiently and sustainably. As customer service executives undergo training and internships, management professionals will also be prepared to lead local branches, helping cooperatives at local, state, and national levels."

Sarah nodded, recognizing the importance of both customer service and management professionals in Peopleism. She saw how AI and IT could be transformative in managing cooperative companies and people organizations.

With her characteristic knack for numbers, Sarah summed up their progress. "By bringing customer service under people's control, we have shifted another 10% to the people's side," she said with a satisfied smile. "That brings us to a 40:60 split. Still in favor of the top 1%"

* * *

Chapter 6

A VISION FOR CONSUMER-OWNED BANK

While Sarah and Atif were brainstorming about sector-specific cooperative companies under the Peopleism model, Sarah introduced an intriguing idea. "You know, Atif, there are two sectors that can't be worker-owned cooperatives but should be consumer-owned cooperatives instead—banking and insurance."

Atif looked puzzled. "Why should consumers own these? I don't get it."

Sarah smiled. "I understand your confusion. Let's imagine a new bank opens. The bank manager invites local people to become customers. Someone comes in and asks, 'Can I get a loan?' The manager says, 'Well, first we need deposits before we can give out loans.' So, the potential customer responds, 'Wait, you're going to use *our* money to lend out loans and make a profit?' The manager replies, 'Yes, we can lend up to 60% of the deposits we have.' The customer says, 'Why do not you lend from your own money?' The manager laughs, 'No, sir, our money is not for lending. We only lend from your deposits.'"

Atif raised his eyebrows. "So, if the person who borrows the money doesn't pay it back, what happens to our deposits?"

Sarah nodded. "Exactly. If enough loans default, the bank could collapse. And what happens then? The depositors lose their money.

The bank may have some insurance, but it often only covers a portion of the deposits. The rest is gone."

Sarah continued, "See, that is the scam. You deposit your hard-earned money thinking it is safe, but it is being used for loans and investments that benefit the bank, while you take on the risk. Plus, banks charge you for everything—account fees, transaction fees—and make a profit from your money. If they fail, it's the depositors who suffer."

Atif looked shocked. "I had no idea banks operated like that. But I know that the bank branches are disappearing and everything is done using technology like ATMs, online, or through a mobile app, but still keep giving convenience fees, transaction fees, and many other fees. On top of that, my money is not safe, and there is no customer service."

Sarah smiled again, "You're not alone. We need a new model—a cooperative banking system owned by the depositors themselves, where their money is protected, and they have a say in how the bank is run."

Atif added, "Yes, there are many banks, cooperatives, or credit unions owned by depositors, but they have failed without technology and professional management. If technology, customer service, and professional management are given to these banks, there is no need for private banks."

To explore the idea further, they decided to meet Rehman, a retired banker who had worked in various positions in both public and private sectors.

The next day, Sarah and Atif sat with Rehman, who had eagerly embraced their idea of Peopleism. When they explained the concept of consumer-owned cooperative banks, he was ecstatic. "That is brilliant," he said. "Private banks are essentially a scam, and government banks are riddled with inefficiencies and corruption. A consumer-owned cooperative bank could change everything."

Atif leaned in, curious. "Rehman, why do you say private banks are a scam? And what's wrong with the current cooperative banks?"

Rehman did not hold back. "Private banks work exactly like Sarah described. They use depositors' money to make loans and investments, and if things go wrong, it is the depositors who lose. Banks charge ridiculous fees, and when they get into trouble, they pass on the risk to the customers."

He paused, then added, "Government banks, on the other hand, are often controlled by politicians. They give out huge loans to failing businesses that never pay them back, leading to huge losses. And who bails them out when they fail? The taxpayers, of course."

Atif asked, "What about existing cooperative banks?"

Rehman sighed. "Cooperative banks are supposed to be owned by the depositors, but the problem is poor management. They lack professional oversight, technology infrastructure, and proper systems. This leads to inefficiency and losses."

Sarah nodded thoughtfully. "So, what would a successful consumer-owned cooperative bank look like?"

Rehman's eyes lit up. "It would be a bank professionally managed by experienced bankers but owned by the depositors. The depositors would elect the board members, and the bank's operations would prioritize protecting their money above all else. No risky investments, no political interference, and no inflated fees."

He continued, "Technology and AI would play a key role. A single national bank with branches across every city, town, and village would operate using advanced tech systems. Whether you're in a village or in a city, the bank would offer the same efficient, automated services. You would have access to your account through mobile apps, online platforms, ATMs, and AI-driven tools that can help with financial decisions, investments, or even taking loans."

Atif nodded. "So, we would not need thousands of banks. Just a national cooperative bank powered by technology, with branches everywhere? Like an electricity utility."

Rehman smiled. "Exactly. The whole system would be tech-driven but human-centered, offering support when needed. AI could be used strategically to assist in transactions, money management, and financial advice. And rather than giving loans directly to individuals, you could lend to sector-specific cooperative companies that would be responsible for offering sustainable loans to workers, keeping everything transparent and safe."

Sarah was convinced. "So, the depositors essentially become shareholders in the bank. They deposit their money, but they also have a say in how the bank is run, electing the board members and influencing key decisions. This keeps the bank accountable to the people who trust it with their money."

Rehman grinned. "Exactly. You would hire professionals like me to manage the bank, but the bank's priorities would be shaped by the depositors—people like you and me. It would be a bank run for the people, by the people."

A New Era for Banking in Peopleism

Sarah and Atif walked away from the meeting with Rehman inspired and ready to move forward. They envisioned a future where banking was not a corporate monopoly but a community-owned, transparent, and professionally managed service.

In this Peopleism model:

1. **Depositors Are Owners**: The people who deposit money in the bank are its shareholders. They elect board members and have a direct say in how the bank operates.
2. **Technology at the Core**: The bank is driven by cutting-edge technology and AI, providing seamless and secure banking services across the nation. Whether online, through mobile, or in person, depositors have access to efficient, secure banking at all times.
3. **Risk-Free Investment**: The bank eliminates risky investments and focuses on protecting depositors' money. Loans are issued responsibly through sector-specific cooperatives to buy income-generating automation, ensuring the sustainability of lending practices.
4. **Minimal Overhead, Maximum Protection**: With technology handling most of the bank's operations, the bank's overhead is kept low. Only 20% of the bank's revenue is used for operational expenses like technology, professional management and customer support.

5. **Support for Income-Generating Loans**: Rather than giving loans to individuals with high risk, loans are channeled through cooperative companies that focus on sustainable, technology and automation based income-generating activities, ensuring economic growth for the whole community.

With this model, Sarah and Atif knew they were onto something revolutionary. A cooperative banking system where the customers had ownership, control, and security—a bank that truly worked for the people.

Sarah exclaimed, "Banking adds another 5% to the people's share, close to the 50% mark. We're now at 45:55, still some distance to go."

Chapter 7

CUSTOMER-OWNED INSURANCE COMPANY

Atif and Sarah were deep into the conversation about consumer-owned financial institutions when Sarah shifted gears, her eyes bright with a new idea. "You know," she began, "the same concept works for insurance—healthcare, general insurance, life insurance, property insurance—it is all the same story. We give money to the insurance companies, they keep most of it, and when we make a claim, they return only a fraction of it, usually no more than 60% of the premiums collected. And to top it off, each claim feels like we are begging for what is rightfully ours, like we are trying to steal *their* money when it is *our* money!"

Atif smiled, sensing Sarah's frustration. "Sounds like you've had a bad experience," he teased.

Sarah nodded. "Oh yes, definitely," she replied. "My brother had a small car accident not long ago. He called the insurance company to get it fixed, and they told him to take the car to a shop. There was a small dent on the other side of the car, so my brother asked the shop to take care of that, too. The shop called the insurance company, and the company's response was that they would treat it as two separate accidents. My brother, not thinking it would matter, said fine. But a few weeks later, he had another accident, a bigger one. This time, when he called the insurance company, they told him they only cover two accidents per year, and he had used up his limit. He had to pay for the repairs out of pocket."

Atif shook his head sympathetically. "That is so unfair. He had no idea!"

"Exactly!" Sarah continued. "There are two things to learn from this. First, my brother had been forced to buy insurance online, without any guidance. If he had an insurance agent, they would have explained the fine print, like the two-accident rule. An agent would have advised him not to file a claim for the small dent and just pay for that out of pocket. Instead, he ended up wasting one of his claims."

"And the second thing?" Atif asked.

"The second thing," Sarah said, her voice more determined, "is that we are giving private companies our money and only getting back a portion of it, with great difficulty. They do not use their own money to cover our claims—they use *our* money. And now, they have even eliminated the one layer of support we had: the insurance agents. They have pushed us to buy insurance online, forcing us to do all the research and legwork ourselves."

Atif leaned forward. "So, what's the solution?"

Sarah smiled. "We need to create our own insurance company, owned by the insured members themselves. Instead of giving our money to a private corporation, we could hire technology, support services, and management services to help us run the company. Imagine this: A technology company provides the AI tools to streamline the entire insurance process. Support service providers help people understand and navigate their policies. A management service provider handles the day-to-day operations of the insurance company. The best part? Since the insured members own the company, the profits are not going to some distant shareholders—they are coming back to us, in the form of dividends."

Atif's eyes lit up. "That is brilliant! You know, in the U.S., I once worked with an insurance consulting firm to help an association of rideshare drivers set up their own captive insurance. The consultant, John Hegarty, explained how large corporations often form their own insurance companies—called captives—to manage the health and vehicle insurance needs of their employees or fleets. He told me it was one of the best-kept secrets for controlling costs and ensuring better claims management."

Sarah nodded eagerly. "That is exactly what we need! But is there a structure for the captives, and do organizations in the US use it for their members? And what did he say the benefits were?"

Atif said, "Hold on. Those are too many questions. Yes, of course, there is a clear structure as to how the insured-owned company works and the regulations. For your question, if the organizations use it. Yes, corporations use it to reduce their burden of employee or fleet insurance, and unfortunately, hardly any people organizations use it because they are not organized. It only works if the consumers are organized. Let me give you the benefits as per my discussion with John."

Atif ticked off the points on his fingers as he explained the benefits of an insured-owned or captive insurance model.

"First," he began, "it gives you *control*. When we run our own insurance company, we can better manage the volatility of premiums. Instead of facing unexpected hikes dictated by market forces, we can set stable rates based on the actual risk profile of our members. Plus, we get to handle claims directly. This means faster resolution, fewer disputes, and, importantly, transparency. No more feeling like you're being cheated out of your money. And then there's the financial side—capturing the investment income and underwriting profits that usually go straight to the insurance company's shareholders. Instead, those profits come back to us, the insured members. We stop being just policyholders and start being stakeholders."

He shifted to the second point. "Then there's *flexibility*. Most insurance companies offer one-size-fits-all policies because they are catering to millions of people. But with a captive or insured-owned insurance company, we can tailor policies to our specific needs. Let's say a group of freelancers wants more health coverage or a community is looking for special property insurance for an area prone to floods. We can design those policies, adjust them, and even introduce benefits that you would not find with a traditional insurer. This also means we have more options for administrative services— we choose how the business operates."

Atif leaned in, emphasizing his next point. "And captives create an *insulated environment*. Since we are not tied to market conditions or the whims of private insurers, we can maintain long-term control over our insurance programs. We're not exposed to the fluctuations that often plague the traditional insurance market, where premiums can suddenly spike because of external factors, like economic recessions or global crises."

He paused for effect before concluding, "The most important part is that this model fosters a sense of *ownership* among the members. When people feel a real stake in the company, they are more likely to act responsibly. This sense of ownership reduces the number of frivolous claims because people know that they are impacting their own costs and benefits. It changes the psychology of insurance—from 'How can I get the most out of this company?' to 'How can we, as a group, ensure the sustainability of this system?' Ultimately, it means fewer claims, better coverage, and a collective reduction in costs."

Sarah nodded, clearly impressed with the depth of insight. "It is not just about the money anymore – it is about empowering people to take control of their own future," she said. "This could change everything."

She added, "Yes, it does. My heart bleeds for the farmers who ensure their crops, and when it comes to claims, they are made to go pillar to post to get their claims approved. Many times, the claims are rejected because of technicalities like the person selling the policy not identifying the right field through GPS or the wrong crop being recorded. Finally, the insurance company makes huge money out of these poor farmers. It will be such a relief for them to own their insurance company."

"Exactly," Atif agreed. "It is about creating a system where people have a stake in the services they use. By organizing an insured-owned insurance cooperative, we could offer policies for health, vehicles, property, crop, life, and all other insurances that are essential for people, all under one roof. The support service representatives would help onboard customers, and those customers would become shareholders first. The technology company would provide AI to streamline claims processing, so there would be no more long, drawn-out battles to get what is yours."

Sarah was already thinking ahead. "And by eliminating the private insurance companies from the equation, we would not just save money on premiums and claims. The insured members would actually *benefit* from the success of the insurance company because the profits, after expenses, would be distributed among the shareholders. They would not just be customers; they would be *owners*."

Atif leaned back, a satisfied look on his face. "That is the future of insurance under Peopleism. The peace of mind that comes from knowing you're not just a number in a system, but a part-owner of it. You would have a voice in how it is run, and you would share in its profits. It is insurance for the people, by the people."

Sarah nodded; her eyes bright with the vision. "Yes, and with the right management services cooperative, we can ensure that the company is run efficiently, fairly, and transparently. It is time to take control of our insurance, just like everything else. It is time for people to own their protection, their peace of mind, and their future."

Sarah concluded with a smile, "We've added another 5% to the people's share of wealth. Now we're equal to the top 1% with a 50:50 split—giving an equal footing for people."

❋ ❋ ❋

Chapter 8

SECTOR-SPECIFIC COOPERATIVE COMPANIES

Sarah had spent countless hours analyzing the intricate connections between technology, job markets, and the service industry. Sharing her findings with Atif, she underscored the urgency of Peopleism in this sector. "The service industry contributes about 60% to the GDP in most countries," she explained. "When you include agricultural and government services, that number rises to 70%. But here is the issue: while it might seem that a corresponding 70% of the workforce is employed in these sectors, in reality, it is less than half and declining. Retail, once a major employer, is being eroded by e-commerce and automated checkouts. Insurance, travel, transportation, and banking are also on track for similar disruptions as AI continues to advance."

Atif nodded thoughtfully. "True, but there will still be opportunities for specialized customer support roles – people who guide consumers through complex processes and provide tailored services."

Sarah agreed but pressed on. "Yes, but even in sectors where human service providers are essential—such as transportation, home services, and construction—automation is set to transform those roles. That is why we need cooperative companies owned by the service providers themselves. As jobs are automated out of existence, the technology that replaces them should be owned by these cooperatives. This way, workers can earn income as shareholders while working fewer hours."

The Structure of Sector-Specific Anchor Cooperative Companies

Sarah leaned in, eyes alight with enthusiasm. "Imagine this: an anchor company for each sector with offices in every city, town, and village, leveraging technology to manage an extensive network of workers and shareholders. It would provide consumers with access to thousands of products and services through the company,

The goods and services would come from multiple providers, but quality and efficiency would be maintained by this one entity."

Atif, always focused on logistics, added, "Overheads would be drastically reduced. Right now, private companies operate with at least 40% overhead—management, IT, customer support, and so on. In a Peopleist system, this could be streamlined to 20%: 5% for management, 5% for technology, and 10% for customer support—all provided by worker-owned cooperatives."

Sarah nodded. "This structure wouldn't just lower prices for consumers; it would redirect most of the revenue to the workers who own the company—the true creators of value."

Reflecting on current corporate practices, she said, "Take Amazon, for example. It is a marketplace that sells everything but adds minimal value, using a wasteful logistics system to deliver products nationwide, one product at a time. In capitalism, this works because profit is the driver. In Peopleism, IT cooperatives would build platforms, and logistics would be localized to minimize waste."

Reclaiming Control

Sarah's expression grew serious. "This isn't just about money – it's about control. The current system keeps us fragmented. The wealth and power are concentrated in the hands of the few, while the rest of us are so busy trying to survive that we miss the collective power we could wield."

Atif's eyes gleamed with understanding. "That's why Peopleism is transformative. Instead of fragmented small businesses fighting for survival, there would be one anchor company per sector, owned by workers and spread nationwide. These cooperatives would pool resources and compete with private companies on equal footing. The difference? The profits would be shared among the workers, not hoarded by a few executives."

"Consider construction," Sarah continued. "Imagine every construction worker, architect, and engineer owning a stake in a cooperative. They'd have the capital to invest in the best equipment, and every profit dollar after expenses would go back to them."

Atif chimed in, "And management, IT, and customer support would all be handled by other worker-owned cooperatives. Overheads would remain capped, ensuring most of the profits stay with the sector."

Sarah's eyes sparkled. "The best part? Workers would not need to choose between being entrepreneurs and employees—they would be both. They could work for other companies but still earn dividends from their sector-based cooperative. It redefines what it means to be an entrepreneur."

Rewriting the Rules

Sarah laughed softly. "It's ironic. We would use the same tools capitalists do—automation and AI—but flip the script. Instead of concentrating profits in the hands of a few, we would distribute them fairly. Instead of fostering a race to the bottom, we'd create a system where everyone benefits, and for the first time, the income is decoupled from work."

Atif's excitement was palpable. "We would be rewriting the rules. And this time, everyone would have a chance to win."

Sarah leaned back, feeling hope she had not experienced in a long time. Peopleism was evolving from an idea into a tangible solution. It was not just about fixing capitalism; it was about creating an entirely new system where workers did not rely on corporate goodwill but were the decision-makers and owners.

A Different Approach for Manufacturing and Agriculture

"Manufacturing and agriculture require a slightly different model," Sarah noted.

Atif, who had studied e-commerce and retail, explained, "Though distinct sectors, their sales and marketing are service-oriented. Specialized cooperatives could manage these processes, from marketing to consumer support."

Sarah added, "Advertising is wasteful and misleading. The customer service cooperative company could eliminate these costs and offer transparent, informed recommendations. Local cooperative-trained workers would handle post-sale support, ensuring products are maintained and repaired efficiently."

Addressing Import and Export Inefficiencies

"The current import-export system is inefficient and drives up consumer costs," Sarah said. "Imports should fill domestic production gaps, but often, redundant imports and exports coexist, burdening consumers. I saw a country importing 200 tons of sugar while exporting 250 tons. It is absurd."

Atif agreed. "A national cooperative managing imports and exports could streamline this, reducing waste, conserving foreign exchange, and prioritizing essential products."

Transforming Public Companies into Cooperatives

"Public companies and cooperatives have existed for decades but often fail due to bureaucracy and lack of expertise," Atif noted. "They were intended to create jobs but became inefficient."

Sarah nodded. "Public enterprises, managed by bureaucrats with limited sector knowledge, lacked innovation and barely integrated automation. They ran at a minimum."

"Peopleism changes that," Atif said. "Professional management and advanced technology would make these companies efficient. Workers would be shareholders, benefiting from automation and AI improvements."

"In this system," Sarah added, "workers wouldn't fear job loss to automation. Their income would align with technological growth."

A Summary of Impact

"By incorporating AI to reduce waste, making workers shareholders, and ensuring professional management," Sarah concluded, "sector-specific cooperative companies could shift wealth to favor the people, potentially increasing it by 10% and creating a 60:40 split in their favor."

Their discussion outlined a bold vision: cooperative companies that are professionally managed, technology-powered, and worker-owned—promising not just economic efficiency but fairness and empowerment for all. Both decided to work on case studies in at least three sectors to explore how AI and cooperative companies worked in those sectors. After intense discussion, they decided on healthcare, transportation, and agriculture for the case studies.

Healthcare and AI

Sarah realized early on that one of the most profound disruptions caused by AI would occur in healthcare. It was a field close to her heart, and she believed that AI's transformative potential could become a positive force—but only under the framework of Peopleism. In Peopleism, AI would not serve corporate interests but would instead be a tool that enhanced the human side of healthcare, providing better outcomes for patients while respecting the dignity and expertise of doctors. AI could empower healthcare providers, not replace them.

To explore how AI could be integrated into a Peopleist healthcare system, Sarah knew she needed the perspective of experienced doctors—those who had spent years in the field and understood both the limitations and potential of technology. She approached Atif, her longtime collaborator, and he immediately thought of Dr. Shafi and Dr. Rehana, a doctor couple with decades of experience across India, the UK, and Saudi Arabia.

Dr. Shafi was a passionate doctor who believed in compassionate care. Having worked in both private hospitals and rural clinics, he was known for his ethical practice, often treating patients for free and never prescribing unnecessary medications. His wife, Dr. Rehana, was a specialist in psychiatric medicine and counseling, admired for her empathetic approach and integrity. Together, they had witnessed the rapid changes in healthcare, particularly during the COVID-19 pandemic when telemedicine became a necessity.

For them, telemedicine had been a revelation. "It allowed us to focus on what really matters—the patient," Dr. Shafi explained during one of their conversations. "We were not wasting time traveling between hospitals or filling out endless paperwork. We could actually talk to our patients and give them the care they needed, even during a global crisis."

Atif saw the potential for their involvement in shaping healthcare under Peopleism. "Dr. Shafi and Dr. Rehana are not driven by money," Atif explained to Sarah. "If they could make a comfortable living while providing more free care, they would be happy to do it. But they are concerned that AI might replace them entirely."

This concern dominated the conversation when Atif and Sarah met with the doctor couple. Dr. Shafi, in particular, was skeptical. "We keep hearing about AI diagnosing diseases, predicting outcomes, and even performing surgeries. How long until we're no longer needed?" he asked.

Atif, sensing their unease, took a moment to explain how AI could transform healthcare—not by replacing doctors, but by empowering them. "I understand your concerns," he began. "But AI isn't here to take away what you do best. It is here to enhance it. Think of AI as a tool that supports you, not overshadows you."

He continued, "Let's look at some of the AI tools already being developed and imagine how they could fit into a Peopleist healthcare system."

AI-Driven Diagnosis and Decision Support Tools
"First, there are AI systems like IBM Watson Health and Google's DeepMind Health," Atif explained. "These tools use vast amounts of medical data to

assist with diagnoses and treatment plans. For example, Watson can analyze patient records, medical literature, and clinical guidelines to recommend personalized treatments for conditions like cancer. In a Peopleist system, such a tool would not be owned by a corporation but by healthcare providers themselves, ensuring that it serves patients, not profits."

Dr. Shafi, though initially skeptical, nodded as Atif described how AI could assist with complex cases. "I've seen cases where a second opinion from AI might have helped," he admitted. "Sometimes we miss things—especially when we're overworked. If AI could provide real-time suggestions or alert us to something we might have overlooked, it could save lives."

AI-Enhanced Imaging and Diagnostics

Atif continued, "Then there are AI-powered imaging tools like Zebra Medical Vision and Aidoc, which are being used to analyze medical images. These tools can detect abnormalities in X-rays, MRIs, and CT scans faster and sometimes more accurately than human radiologists."

Dr. Rehana, who had seen these technologies in action, shared her thoughts. "During my time in Saudi Arabia, I worked with radiologists who were testing AI tools to read scans. It's incredible how quickly AI can flag potential issues, especially in high-pressure environments like emergency rooms."

Atif added, "In Peopleism, AI would work for you, not the other way around. Imagine an AI system that continuously monitors patient data, analyzes their scans, and flags any issues while you focus on patient care. You'd be able to make more informed decisions without spending hours interpreting results."

AI for Predictive Analytics and Preventive Medicine

Sarah, eager to highlight how AI could improve preventive care, jumped in. "Another area where AI is making strides is in predictive analytics. AI tools like KenSci are helping healthcare providers predict which patients are at risk for chronic conditions like diabetes or heart disease. By analyzing data from electronic health records, wearables, and even genetic information, AI can identify at risk patients before symptoms even appear."

Dr. Shafi's eyes lit up at this idea. "That could be revolutionary in rural areas. We often do not have the resources to monitor patients closely, but if AI could predict who is at risk, we could intervene earlier and potentially prevent serious complications."

'In a Peopleist healthcare system,' Sarah added, 'AI could be used to ensure that everyone—regardless of income—has access to preventive care. Predictive analytics could reduce hospitalizations and improve overall health outcomes, saving both lives and resources.'

AI-Assisted Robotic Surgery

Atif shifted the conversation to surgical innovations. "AI-assisted robotic surgery is another game-changer. Systems like the da Vinci Surgical System are allowing surgeons to perform minimally invasive surgeries with unprecedented precision. AI can stabilize instruments, provide real-time data, and reduce human error during critical procedures."

Dr. Shafi looked thoughtful. "I've heard about robotic surgery. It's impressive, but it seems like it's only available to patients who can afford it."

Sarah saw her opportunity. "That is exactly what Peopleism seeks to change. Under our system, advanced technologies like AI-assisted surgery would be accessible to everyone, not just the wealthy. AI would not be a luxury—it would be a tool for equitable care."

AI for Mental Health Support

Turning to Dr. Rehana's expertise, Atif introduced AI tools for mental health. "There are also AI-driven platforms like Woebot and Wysa, which provide mental health support through chatbots. These tools use natural language processing to offer real-time counseling, helping patients manage anxiety, depression, and stress."

Dr. Rehana smiled, intrigued. "I have heard of these. They are not a replacement for therapy, but they can help patients between sessions or those who do not have access to regular care. AI could definitely fill in some gaps, especially in underserved areas."

Atif nodded. "In a Peopleist system, these tools would be integrated into a holistic approach to mental healthcare. They could provide support while you focus on more complex cases, ensuring no patient falls through the cracks."

AI in Personalized Medicine and Genomics

"Another area where AI is making a huge impact is in personalized medicine," Atif explained. "AI can analyze a patient's genetic makeup to recommend treatments tailored to their specific needs. Tools like Tempus and 23andMe are already using AI to study genetic data and recommend targeted therapies for conditions like cancer."

Dr. Shafi looked impressed. "If we could personalize treatment plans for every patient, especially those with chronic diseases or genetic predispositions, we would see much better outcomes. This could change how we approach treatment entirely."

Atif added, "And in Peopleism, AI would not just be a tool for the elite. Genetic testing and personalized treatments would be available to everyone. AI would help make cutting-edge medicine accessible, not a privilege reserved for a few."

AI for Administrative Efficiency

Sarah, seeing the conversation coming full circle, brought up one last point. "One of the biggest frustrations for doctors is the time spent on administrative tasks—billing, scheduling, and paperwork. AI can handle these tasks, allowing you to focus on patient care. Imagine an AI system that schedules appointments, handles billing, and even communicates with insurance companies. You would be free from the burden of paperwork."

She added, "By having AI work side by side with healthcare support service providers, patients would be cared for compassionately before they even see the doctor, creating a patient-friendly environment that promotes faster recovery."

Dr. Shafi and Dr. Rehana exchanged glances. "That would give us so much more time," Dr. Rehana said. "We spend hours each week on tasks that have nothing to do with patient care. If AI and support service providers could take over those responsibilities, we could see more patients and provide better care."

The Promise of Peopleism in Healthcare

Sarah leaned in, sensing that the couple was beginning to see the potential of AI within Peopleism. "In a Peopleist healthcare system, you wouldn't have to worry about profits driving your decisions. AI would be a tool for compassionate care, not corporate gain. The healthcare system would be owned and managed by the people—by doctors, nurses, and patients. AI would generate wealth for the system, not for shareholders."

Dr. Shafi, who had been skeptical at first, now looked intrigued. "So, AI wouldn't replace us. It would empower us."

"Exactly," Atif said. "And not only that, but medical education would shift too. Instead of training doctors to compete with AI, we would teach them to use AI as a tool—focusing on what machines cannot do, like empathy, complex decision-making, and building relationships with patients."

Dr. Rehana nodded. "This could completely change how healthcare works. Patients would get better, more affordable care, and we would have more time to focus on what really matters."

Sarah smiled. "That is the essence of Peopleism. It is about creating a system where technology supports people, not the other way around."

Atif then explained the cooperative ownership model. "In Peopleism, a cooperative company owned by healthcare service providers—doctors, nurses, technicians, and pharmacists—would control all the technologies and automation. The service providers would continue to be paid for their work, but they would also receive dividends from the profits generated by the AI tools they helped implement. This ensures that even if AI takes over much of the routine work, everyone still earns a fair income."

Dr. Shafi laughed. "So even if AI does most of the work, we'd still get paid?"

Atif nodded with a smile. "Exactly. And in many cases, your income from the AI systems could even surpass what you would make in traditional practice."

As the conversation ended, Dr. Shafi and Dr. Rehana were visibly excited. They promised to reach out to their network of healthcare professionals to discuss how Peopleism and AI could revolutionize the system. Atif and Sarah knew that Peopleism had taken a significant step forward in healthcare. The future of medicine was not one where doctors were replaced but where they were empowered—where AI became a tool for compassion and care in a system built for the people.

Education and AI

Atif and Sarah were sitting in a café, deeply engaged in a discussion about peopleism and the potential of AI in education. Atif, a technologist and an educationist who emphasized the importance of mastering basics to build a strong foundation in engineering, was explaining how AI could significantly enhance teachers' work, especially in remote and underserved areas. Sarah, intrigued but cautious, wanted to understand how AI would collaborate with teachers to bring about meaningful change.

"I keep hearing all this hype about AI in education, but I'm a bit skeptical," Sarah admitted. "People talk about it like it's going to fix everything. But how can it actually help in places where we are struggling with even basic resources? And if it is going to replace teachers, I think that could ruin the whole system. AI needs to work *with* teachers, not against them."

Atif nodded thoughtfully. "That's a fair question, Sarah. AI has incredible potential, but it is not a magic solution. Think of it as a tool to amplify what teachers already do, especially in hard-to-reach areas. Imagine a remote village where one teacher is managing multiple grades. AI could support that teacher by personalizing lessons for each student, helping to bridge the gaps when the teacher is overwhelmed."

"Personalizing lessons… how would that work in a real-world setting?" Sarah asked, leaning in.

"Take, for example, a student named Maya in a small mountain town who's struggling with basic maths," Atif explained. "The AI platform she's using would pick up on this and adapt her lessons to focus more on foundational maths skills before advancing to tougher topics. Meanwhile, her friend Ali, who is doing fine in maths but needs help with English, would get different content. Each student gets the support they need without adding to the teacher's workload."

Sarah's eyes lit up. "So it is like having a virtual assistant for each student! That is amazing. But how does that benefit teachers?"

"In a big way!" Atif replied. "Teachers often spend hours trying to figure out where each student is struggling and creating custom materials. AI can handle that assessment part—analyzing student performance and suggesting specific exercises. This frees up teachers to focus on more direct interaction, building relationships, and mentoring students rather than getting bogged down by repetitive tasks."

Sarah smiled, clearly impressed. "I love the idea of giving teachers more time for what really matters. But what about connectivity issues? In many rural areas, they barely have reliable internet. How would AI work in places like that?"

"There are solutions for that too," Atif said. "Some AI platforms are designed to work offline. They download lessons when there's internet access, even briefly, and then work offline so students can study anytime. When the device reconnects, it syncs the data. This way, students do not miss out on adaptive learning even if their internet is spotty."

"That's clever!" Sarah remarked. "So, students don't lose out, even in remote areas. But tech often feels like it is trying to replace teachers rather than support them. How do we ensure teachers stay involved and don't feel sidelined?"

"That's a critical point," Atif agreed. "Good AI in education isn't about replacing teachers; it's about supporting them. For instance, some

AI platforms provide teachers with insights into each student's progress. If a teacher notices that three students are struggling with the same maths concept, AI can highlight that for them. The teacher can then address it right away by adjusting the day's lesson or providing extra support."

Sarah gave a sigh of relief. "So, it is not just about automating things – it is about giving teachers useful insights they can act on. Like having a spotlight on areas that need attention."

"Exactly," Atif replied. "And AI can also make it easier for teachers to access resources. Imagine if an AI system picks up that many students in a class who are struggling with fractions. It could suggest relevant lesson plans, videos, or activities that the teacher could use or customize. It's like having a personal assistant dedicated to helping teachers be as effective as possible."

"It is almost like teachers have a partner in the classroom—even if it is a digital one," Sarah said with a laugh.

"Yes! And it is not just for classroom teaching. AI-powered professional development tools can keep teachers updated on the latest methods and techniques, even in remote areas. Teachers can access virtual coaching from experienced educators worldwide or get resources they wouldn't usually have."

Sarah was visibly excited. "That's brilliant. We talk about bringing quality education to every corner, but this sounds like a way to actually make it happen. Teachers in isolated areas can improve their skills without needing to travel or wait for rare training sessions."

"Right!" Atif agreed. "And don't forget language localization. AI can automatically translate lessons into local languages so students understand better, and teachers do not need to create new materials from scratch. In some places, AI has even translated content into indigenous languages, making learning accessible to even more students."

"That's a huge help," Sarah said, nodding. "Imagine a teacher in a rural village with students who speak a mix of local dialects. AI could bridge that gap and ensure every student understands."

"Exactly. And AI is not just about what happens in the classroom," Atif continued. "Imagine rural students getting to go on virtual field trips—exploring the Amazon rainforest or walking through a museum in Paris. These experiences would be impossible to bring to rural areas otherwise."

Sarah looked amazed. "That's transformative. It is not just about access to information; it is about giving students experiences that broaden their perspectives. But… AI is expensive, right? How do we ensure it doesn't only benefit schools that can afford it?"

"That's a valid concern," Atif acknowledged. "But our Peopleism model ensures that AI and technology are developed by IT professionals and educators, creating affordable or even free AI-based tools for developing regions. Some governments and NGOs are already investing in this because they see education as a great equalizer. With the right partnerships, we can scale these solutions so cost isn't a barrier."

"That sounds promising," Sarah said thoughtfully. "So, AI provides personalized learning for students, practical tools for teachers—even in remote areas—and it's affordable with the right support. If we get this right, it could change everything."

"Absolutely," Atif said with a smile. "It is all about collaboration—teachers and AI working together. AI handles repetitive tasks, frees up time, and provides insights, but teachers bring empathy, creativity, and the human touch that AI cannot replicate. The goal is to make teachers even better at what they do, not to replace them."

"I think I'm starting to get it now," Sarah said, smiling. "Teachers don't have to feel threatened by AI. It's like having a teammate who helps with the heavy lifting so they can focus on what really matters—connecting with students and making a difference."

Also, in Peopleism, everyone who is interested and has aptitude for teaching would get an opportunity, and the teacher cooperative company will be created for all the educators to be part of it and get income from the AI and technology used in education as well as from their own income from teaching. The infrastructure, like schools and colleges, will be part of the national infrastructure, which will be available to every corner of the country, including rural towns.

Reimagining the Transportation Sector

Atif had been mulling over the transportation industry for quite some time. One day, during a discussion, he said to Sarah, "The transportation sector is broken, Sarah. Look at ride-hailing apps like Uber and Lyft. Sure, they disrupted the industry, but at what cost? Commuters are paying through the nose for convenience, and drivers are being exploited with low pay, long hours, and no job security. Once self-driving cars become the norm, it will be even worse. The drivers will be out of work entirely."

Sarah leaned forward, intrigued. "So how would Peopleism change all that? How do we fix the system, especially when technology seems to be driving people out of jobs?"

Atif paused for a moment, collecting his thoughts. "We have to start by looking at transportation from the commuter's perspective. Every day, millions of people rely on different forms of transport to get to work, school, or simply visit family and friends. But no matter the option they choose, the system fails them. Traffic congestion affects everyone. Public transport, while cheap, takes forever. Taxis or ride-shares may be comfortable but are expensive and do not necessarily save time due to wait times. Even using a personal vehicle up to a public transport station and then relying on public transport or ride-shares for the last leg is too complicated and does not really reduce cost or time."

"That is true," Sarah nodded. "Every option has its limitations."

Atif continued, "Now imagine if we used AI to make this process seamless. AI could act like a personal transportation assistant, providing real-time information and connecting commuters to different transportation services—whether it is a bus, a bike-share, a taxi, or even carpooling—based on what is most efficient at any given moment. AI could optimize routes that were previously inaccessible, helping people avoid traffic and cut down on both cost and time."

"Interesting," Sarah said, raising an eyebrow. "But where do the drivers or service providers fit into this? Will not they lose out if AI is doing all the work?"

Atif shook his head. "Not if we apply Peopleism. Here is the difference: instead of having some corporation own all the technology and reap the profits, a cooperative company—owned by the transportation service providers themselves—would manage the AI and the vehicles. The drivers would own the cars they use, or the self-driving cars when that technology arrives. Their income would come not just from providing rides but from owning part of the technology and infrastructure itself. Imagine a driver who no longer needs to spend 10 hours a day behind the wheel but still earns a good income because they are part-owner of the very technology that runs the fleet."

Sarah's eyes widened. "So, drivers will not just be labor anymore. They will be shareholders. That changes everything."

Atif smiled. "Exactly. And as the technology evolves, so will their roles. Even if vehicles become fully autonomous, the cooperative will own the self-driving cars, and the income generated will be distributed to the drivers as shareholders. They may not drive anymore, but they will still be earning a steady income, maybe even more than before."

Sarah leaned in, clearly excited. "So, it is not just about keeping people employed. You're transforming their roles entirely. They will be transitioning from drivers to tech owners."

"That is the vision," Atif agreed. "And it is not just about the vehicles. Think about parking lots and infrastructure. Why should massive parking lot corporations own spaces that don't require much manpower or capital to operate? Those parking lots should also be owned by the transport service providers. When a driver drops off a passenger, they will earn income not just from the ride, but from the parking facilities they own. It is a comprehensive system where everyone involved in the transportation ecosystem—drivers, maintenance workers, even traffic controllers—becomes part of the cooperative."

Sarah smiled, visibly impressed. "This really flips the whole concept of transportation on its head. It is not just about a ride from point A to point B anymore. You're turning the entire infrastructure into a cooperative where everyone earns."

"Exactly," Atif said. "It is a holistic transformation. The transition will be smoother too. If we wait for self-driving cars to be fully implemented by big corporations, drivers will be left jobless. But if they own the very technology that replaces them, they will be able to retire from driving without a drop in income. In fact, they will gain more financial security because the revenue from self-driving cars, parking lots, and even the software that runs the system will be redistributed among them. The key here is ownership and cooperation."

Sarah sat back, clearly inspired. "This is the future of transportation, then. Not just automation, but automation where the profits benefit the workers who are typically left out."

Atif nodded firmly. "Exactly. Under Peopleism, technology will not be the enemy of workers—it will be their ally. Automation does not have to mean job loss; it can mean wealth redistribution. In a cooperative system, the wealth generated by autonomous cars, AI route planning, and even smart parking systems will benefit the very people who used to drive those cars, fix them, and guide commuters. It is a future where technology elevates everyone, not just the shareholders of a few big corporations."

Sarah grinned. "I love it. Transportation is just the start, isn't it? We could apply this model to all sectors."

Atif smiled knowingly. "Exactly. Peopleism is not just about preserving jobs. It is about transforming them and making sure that technology benefits all of us, not just the few at the top."

Transforming Agriculture

Sarah had always been passionate about agriculture, and as she and Atif worked on implementing Peopleism across various sectors, she knew that agriculture was one of the areas most in need of transformation. On a quiet afternoon, as they sat together discussing how Peopleism could revolutionize different industries, Sarah began outlining her concerns.

"Farmers," she said, her frustration clear, "are trapped in an endless cycle of debt. They are dealing with loans, rising costs, unpredictable weather, and market prices that barely cover their expenses. It is no wonder so many are leaving the industry—or worse."

Atif listened carefully. He knew the agricultural sector, especially in developing countries, had become a burden for many farmers. Hearing

Sarah's voice soften, he also understood that the stakes were even higher than he realized. "In many parts of the world," she continued, "farmer suicides are a heartbreaking reality. They cannot see a way out of the system."

She paused, her eyes distant for a moment. "It is not just a crisis of resources. It is a human crisis."

Atif frowned. "But aren't many farmers part of cooperatives? Are not they already working together?"

Sarah nodded, her gaze sharpening again. "Yes, most are part of cooperatives or producer organizations. But they are missing something crucial: access to modern technology. They are still doing everything manually, with no support infrastructure in place. That is where Peopleism comes in."

Rethinking Farming: A New Vision

Sarah's vision was not just about adding software or mechanizing tasks; it was about rethinking the entire structure of farming under Peopleism. She leaned forward, excitement building in her voice. "Agricultural technology is not just about fancy software. It is about combining advanced farming techniques—like vertical farming and greenhouse cultivation—with technology that helps farmers increase their yield, reduce dependency on rain or environmental conditions, and get stable incomes."

Atif nodded, intrigued. "You're talking about innovations like hydroponics and vertical farming, right?"

"Exactly!" Sarah exclaimed. "Take vertical farming, for example. It is the practice of growing crops in stacked layers, often indoors, with controlled environments. This method can produce significantly higher yields than traditional farming, using less water and land. It is ideal for places where arable land is scarce or the climate is unpredictable."

She continued, "Greenhouses, too. Modern greenhouses are not just about covering crops from the weather. They use technology to regulate temperature, humidity, and light, making it possible to grow crops year-round. Imagine a small village in a drought-prone region being able to grow vegetables even during the off-season because they have access to these systems."

Atif was impressed, but he raised a common concern. "But what about the workers? Will not automation and high-tech farming reduce the need for labor, leaving many people jobless?"

Sarah was ready with an answer. "That is the beauty of Peopleism. Instead of replacing workers, we make them shareholders in technology and automation. They become part-owners of the systems that are making farming more efficient. So, even if a machine is doing the planting or harvesting, the income generated from that increased productivity will be shared with the workers. They will make more than they ever did from physical labor alone."

Breaking the Cycle of Exploitation

Sarah's plan was not just about new technology. She wanted to address the structural issues that had plagued farmers for decades. "Right now," she said, "the entire process—from farming to logistics and marketing—is designed to exploit farmers. Each farmer operates in isolation, vulnerable at every stage. They rent transportation, rush to sell their produce before it spoils, and are at the mercy of middlemen who take most of the profits."

Atif was starting to see the bigger picture. "So, what's the solution?" he asked.

Sarah leaned back, her eyes bright with possibility. "Imagine this: a national agricultural services company, supported by an IT backbone, that manages everything—from manpower and automation to logistics and marketing. Farmers would be shareholders in this company, so they directly benefit from the technology. IT professionals and service providers would manage the tech side and earn a capped percentage of the income, while the rest goes to the farmers."

Atif raised an eyebrow, impressed. "You're talking about a total transformation of the industry."

Sarah nodded. "Exactly. And we can fix the pricing system too. Right now, farmers work all year only to end up with prices that do not cover their costs.

Everyone else in the supply chain profits, while the farmer barely survives. Peopleism ensures that farmers get a fair share of the value they create."

A Story from the Field

Atif, now fully engaged, asked, "But do you think farmers will embrace these changes?"

Sarah smiled, remembering a recent trip she had taken to a farming community in Maharashtra. "I visited a village a few months ago. The farmers there were struggling, not because they did not know how to farm, but because they were stuck in an unfair system. One farmer, Ravi, told me about a year when he had a great harvest of onions. He thought he would finally be able to pay off his debts. But by the time he got his onions to market, prices had collapsed, and he sold at a loss. All his hard work, wasted."

Atif shook his head. "That's devastating."

"It was," Sarah agreed. "But here is the thing: Ravi and his fellow farmers were ready for change. They were already part of a cooperative, but they lacked the infrastructure and technology to store their produce and get a fair price. When I explained how Peopleism could help—how they could store their produce in local facilities, use AI to predict market trends, and sell directly to buyers without relying on middlemen—they were excited. They could see how it would work because they were already working together."

Atif nodded thoughtfully. "So, the key is giving farmers the tools they need to control the entire process?"

"Exactly," Sarah said. "With local storage, AI-powered quality control, and direct access to buyers, farmers would no longer be at the mercy of the market. They could sell when the price is right, not when they are forced to."

The Role of Technology in Agriculture

Atif was beginning to appreciate the potential. "You know, this reminds me of what we have discussed in other sectors. AI and automation can eliminate inefficiencies and improve productivity, but the key is making sure the people who do the work—whether farmers or IT professionals—are the ones who benefit."

Sarah nodded enthusiastically. "That is exactly what Peopleism is about. We are not just automating tasks to make a few people richer. We are using technology to lift everyone up. In agriculture, that means making sure farmers have access to modern tools—like AI systems that can predict the best planting and harvesting times, or drones that can monitor crop health."

She continued, "Take drones, for example. They can survey large areas of farmland, check the condition of crops, and even identify problems like pest infestations or nutrient deficiencies. Farmers can then act quickly, reducing crop losses and improving yields. Precision agriculture tools can help them use water, fertilizers, and pesticides more efficiently, reducing costs and environmental impact."

"But what about the laborers?" Atif asked. "What happens to them if machines do everything?"

Sarah's answer was simple. "The laborers become shareholders too. Just like in healthcare, the people who work in the fields will have a stake in the technology. They will earn income not just from physical labor but from their share of the profits generated by the increased efficiency of the system. In many cases, they will make more than they ever did as laborers."

The Cooperative Future of Agriculture

Atif could see the potential unfolding. "So, in this model, the entire community benefits—farmers, workers, service providers—everyone."

"Exactly," Sarah said. "We are creating a system where farmers are not just surviving season to season. They are part of a cooperative, owning the technology that makes their work more efficient and profitable. The profits do not go to some distant corporation; they go back to the people who do the work."

Sarah paused for a moment, then added, "And there's more. With the right technology in place, we can even help farmers diversify their crops. Most farmers grow the same crops every year because it is what they know, or because they have to depend on the monsoon. But with AI and data analysis, we can help them identify other crops that might be more profitable or more resilient to climate change. Vertical farming, for instance, allows farmers to grow different types of crops in smaller, controlled environments."

Path Forward for Peopleism in Agriculture

As their conversation drew to a close, Atif felt a deep sense of optimism. "Sarah, this isn't just about producing more food – it's about giving farmers control over their livelihoods."

Sarah smiled. "Exactly. We are giving them the tools they need to succeed, not just survive. Peopleism in agriculture is not just about increasing yield or cutting costs—it is about creating a fair, sustainable system where farmers are empowered to make decisions, control their future, and share in the wealth they generate."

Atif leaned back, impressed by the clarity of Sarah's vision. "This could change everything."

Sarah nodded. "And it will. With Peopleism, we are not just transforming farming – we are transforming lives."

And with that, Sarah knew that the seeds of change had been planted. It was only a matter of time before Peopleism took root, not just in agriculture but across every sector of the economy, building a future where technology and human effort worked hand in hand for the good of all.

Sarah exclaimed, "We did it!" With an additional 10% of income from sector-specific company ownership, the wealth distribution shifts to a 60:40 ratio, favoring the people. This gives citizens a clear advantage, with the majority share of wealth reinvested into the community, enhancing economic security and fostering shared prosperity.

* * *

Chapter 9

RECLAIMING PUBLIC INFRASTRUCTURE

Sarah, with vast experience working with international organizations, had long been driven by the mission of creating sustainable income sources for all. Her work often centered on how societies could provide for their citizens in ways that preserved dignity, opportunity, and economic security. One of her major explorations was Universal Basic Income (UBI), a concept that promised a safety net for everyone, regardless of their employment status. However, despite its appealing simplicity, Sarah had grown frustrated with the limitations of the UBI initiatives she had encountered. Most were merely pilot programs, conducted as behavioral studies designed to observe how recipients would spend the money rather than tackling the bigger puzzle of how to sustainably fund UBI on a large scale.

One evening, over coffee, Sarah opened up to Atif about her disillusionment with these UBI pilot projects. Atif, an IT professional she often turned to for insights on technology and economics, listened carefully. Sarah's voice was tinged with frustration as she spoke. "You know, Atif," she said, shaking her head, "it's almost ridiculous—the audacity of the wealthy who fund these pilots just to see what poor people would do with a basic income. And the amounts are usually so meager. A few hundred dollars a month, maybe. It's hardly enough to live on, but it's enough to see some positive results."

Atif raised an eyebrow, intrigued. "Positive results?"

'Oh, absolutely,' Sarah continued. 'Despite the intentions behind the studies, the results were eye-opening. People lived better lives, with less stress, more security, and greater opportunities. They could afford basic needs without the constant fear of losing everything. Some even used the money to start small businesses or further their education. It showed that, given the chance, people thrive when they are not constantly worried about survival.'

Atif sipped his coffee and leaned back in his chair, clearly interested. "So, what is the problem, then? If UBI works, why has not it been implemented more widely?"

Sarah sighed. "The real problem is that capitalist economies cannot figure out how to pay for UBI in a sustainable way. The rich do not want to give up their wealth, and government budgets are stretched thin, often relying on loans from those same wealthy individuals just to keep the system afloat. It is a vicious cycle. The government borrows from the rich to sustain public expenses while the majority of people struggle to get by on meager wages or no wages at all."

Intrigued but skeptical of its feasibility, Atif asked, "Sarah, it is clear that capitalism could use something like UBI to balance out the inequality it creates, but would Peopleism also require UBI? And if so, how could it be funded?"

Sarah had anticipated this question. She had spent years researching beyond the surface of pilot projects, looking for long-term solutions to wealth inequality and economic instability. Confidently, she replied, "The answer lies in two words: Public Infrastructure."

Atif furrowed his brow. "Public infrastructure? You mean things like roads and bridges?"

"Exactly," Sarah said, nodding. "But not just physical infrastructure. I am talking about energy infrastructure and, more importantly, technology infrastructure. These are the assets that create wealth in modern economies. The problem is that in our current system, these assets are privately owned by a small group of corporations and wealthy individuals. They capture all the profits while the rest of us pay to use them."

While studying wealth inequality in capitalist economies, Sarah uncovered a critical insight: the corporate capture of technology, physical, and energy infrastructure was at the core of the widening gap between the rich and the poor. While capitalism has always fostered inequality to some extent, recent trends—especially over the past few decades—revealed that technology infrastructure, unlike its physical and energy counterparts, was driving exponential profits for a select few. This, in turn, was exacerbating wealth inequality at an unprecedented scale.

Sarah explained that physical infrastructure, such as buildings, roads, and energy installations, had long provided the foundation of wealth for businesses and nations. These assets, once built, generated steady revenue for their owners over decades with minimal ongoing investment. "Take buildings, for example," Sarah said. "Once constructed, they require only occasional maintenance and upgrades. The costs of upkeep are small compared to the revenue they generate. A building can yield profits for its owner for 40 to 50 years. Roads, airports, and ports work in much the same way. The initial capital investment is recouped in a matter of years, and thereafter, the asset produces a steady flow of income with relatively little effort."

Sarah noted that the revenue from these physical infrastructure assets, after paying off the initial construction costs, could be as much as 15 to 20 percent annually—a reliable return over decades of use. "Energy infrastructure follows a similar trajectory," she continued, "especially renewable energy sources like solar and wind. Once installed, solar panels and wind turbines generate power, and hence revenue, for their owners for 25 to 30 years with minimal upkeep."

Atif nodded, beginning to grasp the broader picture. "So, physical and energy infrastructure provide stable, predictable income for those who own them. But do you know the technology and AI infrastructure. Different from physical infrastructure?"

Sarah leaned forward and said, "How different is it?" Atif explained. "Technology infrastructure is where the real game-changer lies. It behaves like physical infrastructure in that, once developed, it can continue to generate revenue over long periods of time with only periodic maintenance and upgrades. But here is the key difference: the scale of profit generated by technology infrastructure far exceeds that of physical or energy infrastructure."

He paused, letting that sink in. "A company that invests $1 billion in technology infrastructure—say, in cloud storage, operating systems, payment platforms, or enterprise resource planning (ERP) systems—could generate upwards of $25 billion in revenue annually from that single investment. That kind of return on investment is unheard of in the world of physical infrastructure."

Sarah's eyes widened in surprise. "That's an astronomical return."

Atif nodded. "Exactly. Technology companies, particularly those that control the infrastructure of the digital economy, have managed to capture immense value. And it is not just about profits—it is about control. Only a handful of companies have the resources to build and maintain this infrastructure, and they make it nearly impossible for smaller competitors to challenge their dominance."

"When a smaller company does manage to innovate or challenge the status quo," Atif continued, "the tech giants often swoop in and acquire it, further reinforcing their control. This creates a monopoly-like dominance over critical technology infrastructure, leaving little room for new entrants. Add to that the global nature of technology infrastructure, and you've got an even bigger problem."

Sarah tilted her head. "What do you mean by 'global nature'?"

Sarah explained, "While physical infrastructure—like roads and airports—serves only local or national populations, technology infrastructure serves customers worldwide. A digital payment platform, for instance, can be used by businesses and individuals across the globe. This allows tech giants to tap into an unprecedented global customer base, multiplying their revenue streams far beyond what could be achieved in more traditional industries."

Sarah thought for a moment, then asked, "And how do these tech companies price their products? Is it based on the cost of building and maintaining the infrastructure, like with physical assets?"

Atif shook his head. "Not at all. That is part of the problem. While physical infrastructure pricing often follows a model of cost-plus profit, technology companies price their products and services based on what customers are willing to pay. And because their services have become essential to the functioning of the modern economy—things like cloud computing and digital payment platforms are no longer optional for most businesses—customers are willing to pay a premium for access."

Sarah crossed her arms. "So, they're making huge profits from services people can't avoid using."

"Exactly," Atif confirmed. "But the most disruptive factor of all is AI. While information technology has, up until now, served primarily to increase the efficiency of workers and professionals, artificial intelligence is poised to do much more. AI has the potential not just to make workers more efficient but to replace them entirely. It can handle tasks more effectively than humans in many sectors, and this will have an economic impact across every industry."

Atif explained that traditional capitalism operated on the principle of trickle-down economics, where the wealthy invested in capital and earned profits, and those profits supposedly trickled down to workers in the form of wages. "But with AI," she said, "this dynamic is changing. The profits generated by AI will not come from making workers more efficient - they will come from eliminating jobs altogether. The wealthy owners of tech companies will amass exponentially greater profits but at the expense of displaced workers. The trickle-down effect will not apply anymore because there will not be jobs to trickle-down to."

He paused to let that sink in, then added, "Capitalism, as we know it, is obsolete. The exponential profits generated by AI and technology infrastructure are creating a wealth concentration that will destabilize economies if left unchecked. Governments around the world need to recognize this before it is too late."

Atif asked, "That is the thing about technology and AI. As an economist, you tell me how Peopleism would address this problem. What is the solution in your model?"

Sarah smiled. She had been waiting for this question. "It begins with what I call an 'Asset Management Company," she said. "Every country should have one, owned by its citizens."

Atif looked puzzled. "An Asset Management Company? Like BlackRock?"

"Exactly," Sarah said. "BlackRock is the largest asset management company in the world, managing over $10 trillion in assets. It does not produce anything or sell anything—it simply manages assets on behalf of its shareholders, who profit from the returns."

"'But in Peopleism," she continued, "the country's Asset Management Company would be owned collectively by the people. It would manage key public assets—physical infrastructure like roads and bridges, energy infrastructure like solar farms and wind turbines, and technology infrastructure like cloud servers, AI platforms, and payment platforms. The profits from these assets would be distributed to all citizens in the form of Universal Basic Income, free healthcare, education, and other public services."

Atif was intrigued but still had questions. "So, the idea is that citizens would receive income from these public assets, instead of all the profits going to corporations?"

"Exactly," Sarah affirmed. "The income generated by these assets would belong to the people. It is a way to ensure that as AI and automation take over more jobs, people still have a source of income. Instead of a few tech billionaires controlling all the wealth, it would be distributed more equitably. This would stabilize the economy and prevent the kind of inequality we are seeing today."

Sarah went on to explain that several countries already had models that resembled this vision. "Norway, for example, has its sovereign wealth fund, which invests the country's oil profits on behalf of the citizens. The returns from that fund help pay for public services and social welfare. In Alaska, the Permanent Fund Dividend does something similar, distributing oil revenues to residents each year."

Atif's skepticism softened. "But how do we get there? How do we take assets away from the companies that own them now and put them in the hands of the public? Tech companies and the owners of physical and energy infrastructure will not just give up their assets willingly."

Sarah nodded, acknowledging the difficulty. "We are talking about only public assets. The private assets we do not touch. Even then, it will not be easy. Government-owned assets and infrastructure in most countries are still owned by the government but leased or given on contract to the private sector. The lease is usually 30 to 50 years, and we do not have to take the assets back; you just need to end the lease and transfer them to the asset management company. The professionals or worker-owned companies in that sector will manage the assets with management fees. The rent and profits from the infrastructure and assets go directly to the people as income. If we allow the current system to continue, the majority of people will be left jobless and impoverished, while a small elite controls all the wealth and resources."

Sarah said, "Also, we need additional infrastructure for peopleism to make sure that everyone's essential needs are taken care of and provide a basic income for the people."

Sarah said, "I will be exploring the core infrastructure that each country would need to create a sustainable income for all. Atif, you concentrate on technology infrastructure." They began outlining the essential infrastructure for a Peopleist society. Sarah leaned forward; her eyes bright with conviction. "Atif, we need to establish three primary pillars: Technology, Physical, and Energy. And these assets must be publicly owned so that their income can support free healthcare, education, and a basic income for every citizen."

Atif nodded thoughtfully, agreeing that he would focus on technology infrastructure while Sarah would delve into the physical and energy requirements.

A few days later, Atif returned, excitement lighting up his face. "Sarah," he exclaimed, "I knew technology had potential, but the scale of income these assets could generate is incredible!"

He laid out his vision for the foundational technology infrastructure that would empower the people.

Technology Infrastructure

- **Data Centers and Cloud Storage** - "This," Atif began, "is the backbone. Every piece of technology, every platform, and all national data needs a secure place to be stored. Right now, private companies own these cloud infrastructures in most countries. Not only does this mean enormous profits flow to them, but it also poses national security risks if there's even a 0.01% downtime. The people must own this infrastructure, and it should be managed by skilled tech professionals within the country, not corporations with no local accountability."

- **AI Infrastructure** - Atif's voice grew intense. "AI is where the real power lies. Platforms that create and support AI tools, especially sector-specific AI, are tremendously profitable but currently benefit only a handful of global corporations. If we want the income from AI to go to the people, these platforms need to be national assets. Moreover, keeping them under public ownership ensures they cannot be weaponized against citizens or misused by governments."

- **Communication Infrastructure: Spectrum and Telecom Towers** "Communication is essential for every person and business. Our spectrum and telecom towers, managed by private companies, should instead be owned by the people. Public ownership would lower costs for citizens and create substantial income."

- **Banking and Financial Transaction Platforms** - "These platforms facilitate trillions in transactions daily. Imagine if their profits were returned to the people. Instead of private financial tech companies reaping all the benefits, the nation could collect dividends from each transaction made."

Atif paused, looking at Sarah, who was visibly impressed. "Atif, this is brilliant," she said. "And now, let me show you what I found in the realm of physical and energy infrastructure."

Physical Infrastructure

Sarah began, "We already own much of the traditional infrastructure—roads, airports, ports, and government buildings. But we need to expand and modernize these to make sure they are not just functional, but also income-generating for everyone."

- **Technology Service Centers and Community Hubs** - "These centers would offer essential services, including internet access, learning spaces, telehealth, co-working areas, and even childcare, available to everyone. They would generate revenue through membership fees, educational workshops, and rental spaces, ensuring income streams while building community bonds."

- **Warehouses and Cold Storage Facilities** - "In every city, from farms to homes, there's a need for storage. Publicly owned facilities could create income by serving farmers, small businesses, and local cooperatives, who often need affordable storage solutions."

- **Commuter Park-and-Ride Centers** - "With a well-organized commuter system, people will be less dependent on private transport. These centers could earn income through subscriptions and daily fees while reducing congestion and pollution."

- **Public Transport and Rideshare Centers** - "People often depend on private rideshare companies, which collect massive profits. Publicly owned rideshare and transport centers could ensure reliable service at lower rates, with revenue cycling back to the people."

- **Healthcare facilities**—"Hospitals, clinics, testing centers, and telemedicine centers should be available in every village, city, and town. The physical infrastructure is crucial for the country to provide good healthcare to everyone. The rent for these will be paid from the healthcare budget to the asset management company that owns these facilities, and the income can be provided to the people.

- **Schools and colleges** – "Well-equipped, AI-supported schools and colleges' availability in every town and city would ensure that quality education can be provided in every nook and corner of the country. The rent and technology infrastructure cost are given from the education budget to the asset management company.

- **Industrial Parks with Automation and Machinery** - "These parks could host new startups, cooperatives, and independent creators, providing shared access to expensive machinery. They would generate income from user fees while lowering barriers to entry for small enterprises."

- **Local Markets and Cloud Kitchens** - "Marketplaces and cloud kitchens would support local sellers and small food vendors, earning income from leases and transactions. This would boost the local economy, keep food prices affordable, and support budding entrepreneurs."

Energy Infrastructure

Sarah continued, "Finally, energy infrastructure is the lifeblood of modern economies. It's crucial for everything we do, and owning it is key."

- **Renewable Energy Sources** - "Solar, wind, waste-to-energy, and natural gas should all be in public hands. These energy sources not only create essential power but are also excellent revenue streams. Profits from renewable energy projects could directly fund public services, ensuring a clean, reliable energy supply while keeping citizens' utility costs low."

- **Energy Storage and Distribution Networks** - "To make renewable energy more viable, we also need efficient storage and distribution. This will prevent private monopolies from controlling power supply and creating artificial shortages or price hikes."

Sarah finished her report. "These assets alone could provide a strong income base," she said. "In a world with decreasing traditional jobs, this is our way forward."

Funding the Vision

Atif, still thoughtful, asked, "It's wonderful, but where will we get the initial investment for all this?"

Sarah's eyes sparkled. "Natural resources," she replied. "Every country has resources—minerals, forests, oil, gas—many of which are currently handed over to private corporations. Reclaiming these for public benefit could generate enough revenue to fund this infrastructure. The profits from our natural resources should be reinvested in assets that directly serve and enrich people, not shareholders."

She paused and then added, "The key is public awareness. People need to understand that the current system is unsustainable. We must start organizing now, advocating for policies that shift ownership of these critical assets to the public. We need to push for regulations that cap profits from technology infrastructure, reinvest revenue into public goods, and break up monopolies. We need to frame this as a moral issue – an issue of fairness and economic justice."

Atif, seeing the bigger picture, leaned forward with renewed interest. "It's not just about fixing capitalism—it's about evolving it into something new. Peopleism is a way to harness the power of AI and technology for the benefit of all, not just the privileged few."

Sarah smiled, satisfied that her message had resonated. "Exactly. Peopleism is not about eliminating capitalism; it is about evolving it into a system that works for everyone. The wealth generated by technology does not have to be concentrated in the hands of a few. It can be shared equitably, ensuring that no one is left behind in the new economy. AI and automation can create prosperity for all, but only if we choose to distribute that prosperity fairly."

As they wrapped up their conversation, Atif felt a deep sense of hope. Sarah's vision of collective ownership offered a path forward—a way to transform a system that was hurtling toward inequality and instability into one that provided security, opportunity, and dignity for all. It was bold, revolutionary, and ambitious. But more than anything, it felt possible. Atif was ready to be part of that change.

Sarah finally said, "With infrastructure ownership funded by natural resources and other public funds, directing 20% of annual wealth-generation toward the people, the balance shifts decisively in favor of the 99%. This 80:20 ratio gives the majority a sustainable advantage, creating a level of income inequality that is finally manageable."

* * *

Chapter 10

MATERIAL RESOURCES

A tif and Sarah had spent countless hours exploring the intricacies of economic systems, their conversations often wandering through the maze of capitalism's failures, corporate greed, and the inevitable consequences of unchecked inequality. Today, their discussion had reached a new level of urgency, with Sarah focusing on one of the most fundamental questions of wealth distribution: Why were so many countries rich in natural resources still plagued by poverty?

The answer, as they both knew, was embedded in the way global capitalism functioned. The resources—whether it was coal, oil, copper, or rare earth metals—belonged to the people, but they were systematically plundered by multinational corporations with the complicity of corrupt governments. Sarah, with her deep knowledge of global economies, decided it was time to walk Atif through her analysis, one that would shed light on why this injustice persisted and how it could be resolved.

"Atif," Sarah began, "who do you think owns the natural resources in a country—coal, iron, copper, or oil? Is it the government or the people?"

Atif did not hesitate. "The government, obviously. They manage it, right?"

Sarah gave him a knowing smile. "That is what most people think. But here is the thing—the government does not own the resources.

The people do. The government is just a manager tasked with ensuring that these resources are extracted, processed, and sold in a way that benefits the citizens. But do you think that is what is happening?"

Atif's brow furrowed. "I always assumed the government was acting in the people's best interest. But if they're the managers, why do countries rich in natural resources have so much poverty?"

Sarah's eyes darkened as she leaned forward. "That's exactly the problem. The government is not doing its job. Instead of managing these resources for the people, they are selling or leasing them to private multinational corporations, who then extract the resources and keep the lion's share of the profits. The citizens, who should be the rightful beneficiaries, are left with nothing."

Atif looked stunned. "So, you're saying the corporations are essentially stealing the resources?"

"In a sense, yes," Sarah replied. "They enter into deals with corrupt governments, often in developing countries, and acquire the rights to these valuable resources at throwaway prices. Once they have got control, they extract as much as they can, making enormous profits while giving almost nothing back to the country or its people. It's exploitation on a global scale."

"But isn't that just how capitalism works? These companies have the technology and expertise to extract the resources. The governments do not, right?" Atif's question revealed the deeply ingrained assumptions that capitalism had taught him.

Sarah shook her head. "That's what they want you to believe. But it is not true. The companies that own or lease these resources often do not even do the extraction themselves—they hire subcontractors and professional companies that actually have the machinery and expertise. So why can't the government do the same thing? Why can't they hire professionals and keep the profits for the people?"

Atif was silent, the implications of Sarah's words sinking in. He had never thought about it this way. If the government could simply manage the extraction process, why were they handing over control to corporations?

Sarah answered the question he had not asked yet. "It's all about corruption, Atif. Governments—especially in developing countries—

are often more interested in making quick money for themselves than in protecting the interests of their citizens. They sell off the rights to these resources for a fraction of their worth, and the multinational corporations walk away with billions in profits. The people, meanwhile, remain poor, despite living on land that is rich in resources."

Atif felt a wave of anger rise in him. "So, it's not just about greed – it's corruption on both sides."

"Exactly," Sarah said. "And it is a vicious cycle. These corporations, which are already immensely powerful, use their wealth to influence governments, ensuring that they continue to get access to resources at rock-bottom prices. They control entire economies this way. And the people who live in these resource-rich countries? They get nothing."

Sarah paused, letting her words sink in. She knew this was difficult for Atif to digest. After all, capitalism had long sold the idea that wealth would eventually "trickle-down" to the people. But in reality, the wealth was being funneled upwards—into the hands of a tiny elite who controlled both the resources and the political systems that should have been serving the people.

Atif asked the question that had been burning in his mind. "But how can we fix this? How do we stop the corporations from robbing people of their natural resources?"

Sarah smiled. This was the moment she had been waiting for. "That's where Peopleism comes in."

Atif's eyes lit up with curiosity. "Go on."

Sarah explained, "Under Peopleism, the natural assets will be part of the asset management company. We remove the government as the sole manager of these resources. Instead, we create professional, cooperative companies whose sole mission is to manage the extraction for a fee and sale of these resources on behalf of the people."

Atif leaned forward, intrigued. "So, the people would own the resources and the means of extracting them?"

"Exactly," Sarah said. "And because these resources are finite—once they are gone, they are gone—it is crucial that we use the profits wisely. We cannot just give everyone a lump sum of money and call it a day. Instead, we reinvest the profits into building essential infrastructure—things like renewable energy projects, technology and AI infrastructure, healthcare, and education infrastructure. This way, we create long-term, sustainable wealth that will benefit future generations, even after the natural resources have been depleted."

Atif was beginning to see the potential of this system. "So, it's not just about redistributing wealth – it's about creating a system that benefits everyone, now and in the future."

"Exactly," Sarah said. "Peopleism is not just about taking power away from corporations – it is about giving people control over their own future. The wealth generated from natural resources would be used to build infrastructure that supports economic growth, creates jobs or income, and ensures that everyone has access to the basic necessities of life."

"But how do we stop the corporations?" Atif asked. "How do we prevent them from continuing to exploit these resources?"

Sarah's face grew serious. "It won't be easy. These corporations are incredibly powerful, and they have been playing this game for a long time. But the first step is to educate people—to make them aware of what is happening and to show them that there's another way. We need to build a movement, both on a national and global scale, that demands change. And we need to create laws and policies that prioritize the well-being of citizens over the profits of corporations."

Atif nodded. "So, it's about building awareness, creating a system that works for the people, and pushing for political change."

"Exactly," Sarah said. "And we cannot rely on governments to do this for us. In many cases, they are part of the problem. That is why Peopleism is about decentralizing power—taking control away from corrupt governments and corporations and giving it back to the people."

Atif was quiet for a moment, thinking. "It sounds like a revolution – a peaceful one, but a revolution nonetheless."

Sarah smiled. "It is. And it is long overdue. For too long, the wealth generated by natural resources has been funneled into the hands of a few, while the people who should have been the beneficiaries are left with nothing. Peopleism changes that. It creates a system where everyone benefits, not just the elite."

Atif felt a surge of hope. "Do you really think it's possible?"

Sarah nodded. "I do. It will not be easy, and it will not happen overnight. But if we can build enough awareness, if we can get enough people to understand what is at stake, then yes, it is possible. And it is necessary. Because if we do not change the way we manage our resources—if we allow corporations to continue exploiting the earth for their gain—then we are headed for disaster."

Atif considered the implications of Sarah's words. He had always believed that capitalism, for all its flaws, was the best system we had. But now, he was starting to see things differently. Maybe it was time for a new system—a system that put people first rather than profits.

Sarah could see the change in him. "It is a big idea, I know," she said gently. "But it is the only way forward. If we do not take action now, the gap between the rich and the poor will continue to grow, and the consequences will be catastrophic. Peopleism is our chance to build a better future—a future where resources are managed for the benefit of everyone, not just a privileged few."

Atif nodded slowly, feeling a new sense of purpose. "You're right, Sarah. It's time for a change."

Sarah smiled. "Welcome to the revolution, Atif."

* * *

Chapter 11

DEMOCRACY, GOVERNMENT AND PEOPLEISM

In the growing discourse on democracy's decline, Sarah had spent sleepless nights poring over data, watching the steady degradation of democratic structures across the world. It was grim. As the results poured in, she looked at Atif, her face reflecting the weight of the information she had gathered. "Democracy is deteriorating in most countries," she said, her voice measured. "Many are falling into partial democracies where the rule of law is fragile, and representatives no longer represent the will of the people. Politicians and bureaucrats have become disconnected from the needs of citizens."

Atif leaned back in his chair, processing her words. "But why?" he asked. "Aren't elections still happening? Don't citizens vote properly? Is social media and mass media influencing them so much that they believe whatever the politicians say?"

Sarah sighed; her research laid out before her. "The problem is deeper than that," she said. "It is not just about voting or being swayed by media narratives, although those factors play a role. The real issue lies in the manipulation of elections and how representatives, once elected, act as though they are monarchs—kings and princes—rather than public servants. They make decisions that often go against the interests and desires of the majority. During election campaigns, they present grand promises, but once elected, they find a hundred different ways to avoid fulfilling those promises."

"That sounds like cronyism," Atif remarked, shaking his head.

"Exactly," Sarah responded. "Crony capitalism is another major culprit. Industries and private companies have infiltrated the political system, influencing government decisions to suit their own interests. Elections have become exorbitantly expensive, and who do you think funds them? Private corporations and industry associations, entities that should not be involved in the political process, are pouring money into elections. And in return, they receive policy favors, tax breaks, and government contracts."

Also, think about the way they are squandering our natural resources and infrastructure by selling off public companies and material resources. If the natural resources are properly used for the benefit of people, there will be no poverty in any country. The major culprits are our elected representatives and bureaucrats.

Atif frowned. "That is concerning. And then there's the issue of free speech. It seems like governments are cracking down more and more on dissent."

Sarah nodded gravely. "Exactly. The freedom of speech, the fundamental right of citizens to express themselves and challenge authority, is under siege. Governments devise more and more regulations to curb dissent, labeling it dangerous or unlawful. The pandemic was a prime example of how governments imposed restrictions under the guise of public safety, isolating people in their homes, enforcing mask mandates, and promoting half-baked vaccines without allowing open scientific debate. Travel restrictions, quarantine measures—many of these rules were enforced without proper scientific backing."

Atif, always a pragmatist, interjected. "But weren't those curbs necessary? Did not they come from institutions that have been studying viruses for decades?"

Sarah was prepared for this. "Yes, but those decisions were not solely based on public health. They were influenced by private pharmaceutical companies looking to profit from the crisis. Now, we are learning that the vaccines did not prevent transmission as effectively as advertised, and they came with side effects that were downplayed. Despite this, the pharmaceutical companies refused to waive patents to make vaccines more accessible to poorer nations. Governments, in many cases, funded the vaccine research, but the people received no concessions or benefits. It is a clear example of how even democratic governments no longer prioritize the welfare of their citizens."

Sarah paused for a moment before continuing. "This will change in Peopleism. Our system will be built to prevent these kinds of abuses."

Atif raised an eyebrow. "How exactly? How will Peopleism fix these problems?"

Sarah smiled, having anticipated the question. "First and foremost, in Peopleism, the government and officials will be kept away from controlling natural resources and infrastructure. These will be owned by the people, with experts among them making decisions on their use. Then we address how we elect our representatives. Elections in Peopleism will be fair. Whether machines or ballot papers are used, Customer Service Reps will ensure that no fraud occurs, and citizens are protected from manipulation. Election commissions in each country will function as service providers, while complaints and oversight will be handled by Customer Service Reps, who represent the people, not the state." Atif was impressed. "So, you're saying that elections, like other services, will be managed by the people through their representatives—the Customer Service Reps?"

"Exactly," Sarah responded. "The IT infrastructure that supports elections—like voting machines, databases, and information systems—will be managed by IT service cooperatives owned by professionals. Political parties or corporations will not sway these professionals. They will be responsible for developing, maintaining, and securing election systems, while Customer Service Reps will oversee the entire process to ensure transparency. Candidates will not need their own party workers to monitor the machines or guard against manipulation. This kind of fear and fraud must be stopped at its root. Customer Service Reps will ensure a transparent process, from issuing and updating voter IDs to casting and counting the votes," she went on. "We will also introduce the AI Citizen

App, a platform that will provide voters with comprehensive information about each candidate, their party, and their manifesto. After the election, citizens will receive real-time updates about government decisions, policies, and developments through the app. This way, there will be no secrecy. If the government strays from its mandate, citizens will know."

Atif leaned forward, clearly intrigued. "That is a game-changer. But what if representatives still don't perform? What if they betray the people's trust?"

Sarah was ready for this question too. "In Peopleism, the right to recall will become a mandatory part of governance. If a representative fails to live up to the expectations of their constituents, the people will have the power to recall them and initiate a new election. No more waiting for years to correct a bad decision. Accountability will be immediate and enforceable."

"That is revolutionary," Atif said, nodding. "What about the lavish spending on elections, the luxury lifestyles of politicians, and their multiple pensions? How does Peopleism handle that?"

Sarah's expression hardened. "All of that will be curtailed. The fanfare, the extravagant spending during campaigns—it will all be unnecessary. Elections should be about ideas, not pageantry. Representatives of Peopleism will live modest lives in line with the citizens they serve. They will be accessible to the people at all times, not hiding behind layers of bureaucracy. Public office will no longer be a path to personal wealth."

Atif thought for a moment. "And what about the bureaucracy? Government institutions are notorious for inefficiency and corruption. How do we deal with that?"

Sarah smiled. "That is a good question. In Peopleism, the role of government will be significantly reduced, and the elite status of bureaucrats will be diminished. The Customer Service Reps will act as the interface between the government and the people. They will be responsible for holding government officials accountable, ensuring that services are delivered efficiently and transparently."

She continued, "Right now, government service providers are not accountable to anyone. There's no support mechanism for people to question their inefficiency or corruption. Customer Service Reps will form that support layer, representing the interests of the people and making sure that government services are delivered properly. The technology that powers government operations will be provided by IT service cooperatives, ensuring that the systems are secure, efficient, and free from corruption."

Atif nodded. "So, the government services, which are essential to the people, will be managed by professionals who are invested in the well-being of the community, not just their own profits. That is a radical shift."

"Exactly," Sarah said. "Peopleism is about protecting the interests of the people, and that includes ensuring that government services are accessible and of high-quality. There will be no compromises when it comes to the delivery of essential services."

Sarah and Atif sat in silence for a moment, reflecting on the enormity of the changes they were discussing. Peopleism was not just a new economic model; it was a complete reimagining of how democracy and governance could work for the people rather than for the powerful few.

"Peopleism will return power to where it belongs—with the people," Sarah said finally. "It's not about dismantling government or democracy, but about making them work the way they were always meant to: in service of the citizens."

Atif, still deep in thought, murmured, "This could change everything."

"It will," Sarah responded with quiet determination. "It has to."

Atif smiled, feeling a flicker of hope. "You know what? Let's see how Peopleism could change Indian politics."

Sarah raised an eyebrow, intrigued. "Indian politics? That is a big topic, but I am all for it. What do you have in mind?"

Atif, though a global citizen with experience living in various countries, still felt deeply connected to Indian politics. He was concerned about the alarming trends he had been observing in India, particularly how it seemed to be failing in many democratic parameters. "Yes, let's start with India. I am very much interested in how Peopleism can transform the largest democracy in the world because, honestly, it feels like India is slipping into a partial democracy and dangerously close to autocracy."

Sarah nodded. "India is crucial, not just because of its size but because it is supposed to be a beacon of democracy for the world. Yet, in recent years, we have seen a steady erosion of democratic values."

Atif was ready to dive into the details. "The first thing that comes to mind is the deepening crony capitalism. It is taken capitalism to a different level, where it is no longer about free markets but about oligarchic control. This has created massive inequality, with a few individuals amassing enormous wealth while inflation, unemployment, and underemployment are on the rise. The wealth disparity is shocking."

Sarah agreed, her expression serious. "And the government has played a role in this, hasn't it? We have seen close ties between political leaders and major industrialists. It is no secret that these oligarchs influence policy decisions. This kind of crony capitalism undermines the very foundation of democracy."

"Exactly," Atif said, his voice heavy with concern. "This trend has continued for over a decade now, especially under the current regime. Despite failing to address critical issues like job creation and wealth inequality, they are selling off our assets to a select few oligarchs and with the funding from them, they keep coming back to power with ease. This is where elections in India have become incredibly expensive and, frankly, questionable. If we do not address the electoral process first, how can we expect real change?"

Sarah leaned forward, her mind racing with ideas. "Peopleism could fundamentally reshape Indian elections. As we discussed, the introduction of customer service representatives to oversee elections would remove much of the corruption and manipulation. Indian elections have become a spectacle of money and power. With Peopleism, elections would be about policies and ideas, not who has the largest campaign budget."

Atif was encouraged. "And this would stop the flow of corporate money into politics, wouldn't it? Without the corporate funding, politicians will not be beholden to these oligarchs."

"Exactly," Sarah said. "The election process in Peopleism would be transparent and accountable, managed by IT service cooperatives, not private companies or political parties. The AI Citizen App would provide voters with all the information they need—unfiltered, unbiased, and free from the influence of corporate media."

Atif's mind flashed back to Indian politics. "And what about the media in India? It feels like a significant part of the problem. So much of the media is now controlled by corporations or political interests. News is often skewed to favor those in power."

Sarah nodded solemnly. "The media is another pillar that needs reform. In Peopleism, the media would be democratized. Independent journalism would be protected, and the AI Citizen App would act as a direct channel for accurate information, bypassing the influence of corrupt media outlets. Citizens would have access to verified facts and transparent reports on government activities."

"And what about accountability?" Atif asked. "In India, there's growing disillusionment with politicians because they make promises during elections, but once they are in office, they become untouchable. There's no way to hold them accountable for their failures."

Sarah smiled. "That is where the right to recall comes in. In Peopleism, citizens will not have to wait five years to remove a politician who has failed them. The right to recall will be embedded in the system, giving voters the power to remove underperforming representatives and call for fresh elections whenever needed."

Atif was clearly excited. "That would change everything. No more broken promises. Politicians would be forced to deliver or face the consequences."

Sarah continued. "Exactly. And Peopleism would also eliminate the extravagant spending and luxury lifestyles of politicians. In India, we have seen politicians accumulate wealth and live far removed from the everyday realities of the people they are supposed to serve. This has to stop. In Peopleism, public office will no longer be a path to personal wealth but a duty of service."

Atif nodded, his optimism growing. "And the bureaucracy? Indian bureaucracy is infamous for inefficiency and corruption. How does Peopleism address that?"

Sarah leaned back; her eyes sharp with determination. "Bureaucracy in India is a relic of colonial rule, and in its current form, it has become bloated and unaccountable. In Peopleism, the role of bureaucracy will be significantly reduced. Customer Service Reps will act as the bridge between the people and the government, holding bureaucrats accountable. If they fail to deliver services efficiently or transparently, they will answer to the people, not the state."

Atif could feel the possibilities opening up. "And government services? They are essential to the people, especially in a country as large and diverse as India. But they are often plagued by inefficiency and corruption."

Sarah agreed. "That is why the IT cooperatives are key. These cooperatives will provide the technology and systems that run government services. The technology will be secure, efficient, and free from corruption because it will be managed by professionals who are invested in the well-being of the people, not in profit margins."

Atif smiled. "So, in Peopleism, the Indian government would finally serve the people, not the elite few or the bureaucratic machine."

"Exactly," Sarah said. "India has the potential to be a thriving democracy, a true people's democracy, but it needs to break free from the chains of crony capitalism, corruption, and bureaucratic inefficiency. Peopleism offers that path."

They sat in silence for a moment, both contemplating the transformation they had envisioned for India. In the largest democracy in the world, Peopleism could be the solution to restore power to the people and reclaim the democratic ideals that had once inspired the nation.

Atif broke the silence. "This could change everything."

"It will," Sarah said softly. "It has to."

✳ ✳ ✳

Chapter 12

PEOPLEISM IN ACTION – CITY OF DAWN

In the sprawling metropolis of Vishram, a city of stark contrasts, gleaming skyscrapers pierced the skyline, symbolizing both cutting-edge progress and the deep chasm of inequality. Towering office buildings and luxury apartments cast long shadows over the streets below, where most citizens hustled through their daily grind, trapped in a relentless cycle of capitalism. Despite their hard work, the majority of Vishram's people never seemed to catch up, as the wealth of the city flowed into the pockets of a privileged few. These elite, powered by profits from AI and automation, continued to accumulate wealth at an unprecedented pace, creating a city where technological marvels stood side by side with growing economic disparity.

But Vishram was not just a city of glass towers and tech giants. Its other half lay in the rural belt, a vast and fertile region that was as much a part of the city as its bustling urban core. This agricultural expanse provided the lifeblood of the city—fresh fruits, vegetables, milk, and meat that fed its millions of residents. In theory, this unique blend of rural and urban should have created a harmonious system, where city dwellers enjoyed affordable, farm-fresh food, and farmers thrived by supplying a substantial produce to nearby markets.

In reality, however, the supply chain was tangled in a web of middlemen, corporate interests, and profiteering vendors who distorted the flow of goods from farm to table. Instead of reaping the benefits of their labor, the farmers remained impoverished, squeezed by dealers and companies that controlled prices and distribution. Meanwhile, city residents paid inflated prices for food that should have been both cheaper and more accessible.

Yet beneath the surface of this complex metropolis, a quiet revolution was brewing. The Peopleist movement, a new force advocating for fairness, equity, and the redistribution of wealth, was taking root in Vishram. It was poised to turn the old system on its head, offering a radical alternative to the exploitative capitalism that defined the city. Peopleism promised to break the stranglehold of corporations and middlemen, ensuring that the wealth generated by AI, automation, and infrastructure would no longer be concentrated in the hands of a few.

In the heart of Vishram, the seeds of change were being sown. The city's rural belt, once taken for granted, would soon become a symbol of empowerment. Farmers, long at the mercy of dealers, would be uplifted through cooperative ownership and direct partnerships with city residents. AI and automation, instead of serving only the elite, would be harnessed to improve efficiency and fairness in the distribution of food and resources.

As Vishram stood on the verge of this transformation, its streets buzzed with a sense of possibility. The people, tired of working long hours for scraps, were beginning to believe in something greater – a future where the fruits of their labor, and the riches of their land, would finally belong to them.

Sarah, the visionary behind Peopleism, had long dreamed of a world where technology empowered the masses, rather than enriching a select few. After years of research, debates, and tireless advocacy, her dream was about to become reality. Vishram was chosen to be the world's first Peopleist city—a place where the wealth generated by technology would be shared with the workers and where AI would enhance human potential instead of replacing it.

Standing beside her on a rooftop, gazing out at the city, was Atif, a technologist and her long time collaborator. "This is where it begins," Sarah said, her voice filled with anticipation. "Vishram will be the blueprint for the future—a city where the power of technology belongs to the people."

Atif nodded, his mind racing with possibilities. "The stakes are high, but if we succeed, we'll change everything." Sarah, with her economist mindset, was looking at the economy of the City of Vishram. She said, "You know this is the best place to start our peopleism campaign because the economy of the city reflects the economy of the country. It has urban areas; it has rural areas. It has manufacturing, tech companies, and agriculture which reflect the state and country's working population."

Building the IT Support Representative and Management Professionals Network

Atif had always known that technology would be the driving force in implementing Peopleism, and now he had the chance to unite the very people who could drive that change—Vishram's IT, support, and management professionals. Over 2,400 IT and IT-enabled service professionals had already registered through SocialConnect, a platform Atif had developed specifically to organize professionals based on their skills and aspirations. Among them were 930 eager youths, fresh out of university, still searching for their first job after one to three years of waiting. They needed guidance, training, and a chance to prove themselves.

They were the group who would drive the peopleism concept to implementation. Almost 50% were freshers, but the other fifty were veterans with years of experience in the corporate world, government offices, and many were unemployed or laid off after years of service. Some retirees registered enthusiastically to be part of the momentous occasion.

The IT professionals will be trained in developing the IT and AI technology platform and tools required for the smooth management of each sector within the city. Most of the technology existed as open source and based on the feedback over the course of the training and implementation, it will be updated as required. But the AI and automation will be developed as part of the global IT professionals' network and made available to the city of Vishram and later to every country.

The support representatives, all of them would be trained in customer service first and then they choose two sectors of their choice to be specialists. The technology and AI would make their work very easy, but they need to add value as friends of the people. They are trained to help the people without the constraint of time and other limitations. The responsibility of product and service research, using the tools and communicating with the people, was the mainstay of their role.

The management professionals have a bigger role to play. Along with managing the organizations and networks, and facilitating the sales and marketing, and human resource management, the professionals become specialists in two different sectors and will form the management team in those sectors to anchor cooperative companies.

The first step was clear: establish Technology Service Centers in each of Vishram's five communities. With the support of the city's mayor, who saw the potential in Peopleism, Atif secured temporary use of vacant classrooms in the local college as training hubs for IT professionals and support service personnel and management professionals—an interim solution until the new centers were built.

The First Year of Transition

January 1st marked the dawn of a new era for Vishram. Despite being a holiday, excitement was in the air as Sarah and Atif called 2400 IT professionals to the college campus for their orientation. The group gathered in the quadrangle, buzzing with anticipation. Atif had planned a day full of activities, designed to be informal yet inspiring, to set the tone for the Peopleist movement's IT training and internships.

The event kicked off with speeches from the two visionaries who sparked the revolution—Atif and Sarah. Atif took the stage first, setting the tone for the day.

"Building a New Future Together"

Good morning, everyone. Today, as I stand here, I am filled with a sense of purpose and excitement—because we are at the beginning of something extraordinary. We are gathered not just to begin training or start new jobs, but to build a future that will transform this city and the world.

For years, we've seen how technology—something we've helped create—has been used to benefit a few, leaving the rest of us to work harder just to survive. Many of us have been part of that system, building platforms, writing code, solving problems, only to watch the profits go to someone else. Today, that changes.

What we're about to create here in Vishram is the world's first Peopleist city. And you—you, the IT professionals and support service providers and management professionals—are the heart of this revolution. Peopleism is not just a new economic model; it's a philosophy, a way of life that puts people at the center of everything. AI, automation, technology—they will no longer be tools to take away jobs or reduce human value. Instead, they will empower us to live better, more meaningful lives.

Think about this for a moment: the wealth generated by technology will be ours. The choices we make about how technology is used will be ours. We are no longer just workers – we are the leaders, the creators, the owners of our future. This is your opportunity to be part of something that redefines what work and life can look like.

Today, we begin by working together, not as competitors, but as collaborators. In the past, many of us have felt pressure to compete—to outshine one another, to fight for limited opportunities. But here, we change that. We are building a network, a community where each of us thrives by helping each other.

The Technology Service Centers we're building across Vishram will serve as spaces of learning, growth, and collaboration. They will be hubs where ideas flow freely, where you'll train not just to be better professionals, but to be better collaborators—better citizens of a new economic reality.

In Peopleism, success isn't measured by how much you take from others, but by how much you can give back. And the beauty of it is, the more you give, the more you will receive.

I know many of you are eager to begin. Some of you have been waiting for years for a job or an opportunity, and I promise you this: we will not let you down. Over the next few months, you will be learning, working, and experimenting in ways that will not only sharpen your skills but also open your mind to new possibilities.

We'll guide you, but ultimately, this journey is yours to take. And it won't be an easy one. There will be moments of uncertainty and doubt, but I urge you to trust the process. Lean on each other. Use the support systems we've built. This isn't just about personal growth—it's about collective growth.

I'll end with this: Today marks the beginning of a new chapter, not just for you, but for Vishram, for technology, and for how we define work and wealth. You are the pioneers of Peopleism, and your work here will set the foundation for what's to come.

We're not just coding the future – we're creating it.

Thank you.

The audience burst into applause and did not stop until Atif took his seat. With a warm smile, Sarah stood up, acknowledging the energy in the room, and began her speech.

Sarah's Speech

"Shaping an Economy for People"

Good morning, everyone. Standing here today, I am reminded of why we started this journey in the first place. We began with a simple idea: that the power of technology and the wealth it generates should not belong to a select few but to the people who create, maintain, and depend on it.

Peopleism isn't just a new idea—it's a movement that brings hope to a world that has seen far too many people left behind. And today, that movement begins with you.

Look around this city, look at the streets, the buildings, the people. For years, Vishram, like many other cities, has been driven by a system that prioritizes profit over people. We've all seen the results—inequality, frustration, jobs that drain our energy but fail to reward us with meaning or security.

But you know what? It doesn't have to be this way. Technology has the potential to uplift entire communities, to generate wealth for everyone—not just those at the top. That's what Peopleism is all about: ensuring that the benefits of AI and automation are shared fairly, empowering us all to live fuller, richer lives.

And you, as IT professionals and service providers, are the ones who will show the world how this can be done.

Peopleism offers something that capitalism and even socialism couldn't fully grasp: the separation of work from survival. Here, your livelihood isn't tied to the number of hours you clock in or the competition you face in the workplace. Instead, your livelihood is tied to your participation in an economy that you help build, an economy where you are co-owners.

We are not just giving you jobs – we are giving you ownership. You own your time. You own the tools you work with. And, most importantly, you own the direction of your career and life.

What does that mean for you? It means that, starting today, you get to choose. Choose which sector excites you. Choose which role you want to play in this economy. We will give you the support, the training, and the resources you need to make those choices, but ultimately, this future is yours to design.

As Atif mentioned, today is about collaboration. The old ways of doing things—where people are pitted against each other in a race for survival—are over. We are creating a new environment where everyone's success is tied to collective success.

Imagine what we can achieve when competition is replaced by compassion. When instead of tearing each other down, we lift each other up. Imagine a workplace where your growth benefits your colleagues, and their growth benefits you.

This is the essence of Peopleism: building a society where everyone has a place, where everyone contributes in a way that's meaningful to them, and where the wealth of the system flows back to its creators.

We've already seen the potential of what you can achieve. Over 2,400 of you have joined the IT Professionals Network. You've committed to being the first to learn, the first to lead, and the first to build a new economy. In the coming months, you'll be diving deep into different sectors, exploring industries that need your skills and creativity to thrive.

I want you to embrace this moment. This is your chance to shape not just your future, but the future of an entire city, and potentially the world.

You are not just the architects of Peopleism – you are its heart and soul.

In the coming months, we will face challenges. Every revolution does. But we are ready, and more importantly, we are united. In Peopleism, every person matters. Every contribution counts. And every choice you make will help bring us closer to a world where technology serves people, not profits.

Together, we will create a future where compassion, collaboration, and shared prosperity define what it means to work and live.

Thank you.

The audience rose to their feet, their applause echoing through the room. They called for Atif and Sarah to join them, standing side by side as the clapping continued, unwavering and heartfelt. In that powerful moment, Atif and Sarah exchanged a look of quiet pride and deep satisfaction. All the hard work, the sleepless nights, the challenges they had faced—everything had led to this. Their vision was no longer just an idea; it was becoming a reality. The seeds they had planted were finally bearing fruit.

After the speeches, they kicked off with a video presentation Atif had carefully crafted. It laid out how Peopleism would not only reshape their professional lives but also elevate their personal well-being. The message was clear: they were not just learning new skills; they were becoming the first wave of leaders in a revolution that would return economic power to the workers.

The second activity moved away from technicalities and focused on human connections. Dividing the participants into small groups, Atif encouraged them to see each other as comrades, not competitors— quite the opposite of the corporate world where survival often meant undercutting others. Here, they were building a community where cooperation was key and where helping one another thrive was the ultimate goal.

As the day progressed, the orientation took a more technical turn. The professionals assessed their current skill levels, explored their passions, and discussed how they could contribute to the Peopleist movement. After lunch, Atif brought in sector experts for brief video presentations, followed by discussions about the role of IT and AI in various industries, from healthcare to agriculture to public services. Over the next month, the interns would dive deeper into these sectors, rotating through workplaces to find their niche.

The most important message Atif emphasized was freedom: nothing was set in stone. Even after choosing a sector, the interns could switch if they felt another path was more aligned with their interests and values. This flexibility was key to ensuring that no one felt trapped, as they might in a traditional capitalist job.

A New Hope for the Youth

After the session, a group of young professionals, eyes alight with enthusiasm, approached Atif. Shereen, one of the more vocal participants, asked, "Sir, is this real? It feels like we've stepped into an alternate universe."

Atif smiled knowingly. He had anticipated this kind of reaction. "Yes, it's real. Life is simple in Peopleism. Here, the choice is yours—do not do anything you're not passionate about. There's plenty of work, and the economy generates more than enough wealth. Before, that wealth went to the top 1%, but now, we control it. It's not about getting rich at someone else's expense—it's about efficiency, compassion, and using technology for good."

The day ended on a high note, with Sarah joining the discussions, deeply engaged with the sector experts who were now part of this unprecedented collaboration. Together, they were shaping a new world where people, not profits, were at the center.

In Vishram, the future had arrived, and it belonged to the people.

Local residents benefit from Peopleism

The Customer Service Reps, the customer service representatives, were given options to learn 2 to 3 sectors, with the first sector being just customer service, including connecting with the local residents. Connecting with the local residents was a building block of the customer service representative's journey from just doing their job to becoming a Customer Service Rep or friend of the people. It is essential for the Customer Service Reps to interact with the people over the phone or face-to-face in the service center or by reaching out to them at the homes of local residents. Remember, there is no time constraint, they are not selling anything, and they are as compassionate as possible. This training was 3 months long, and surprisingly, we realized that the youth from rural areas more naturally handled it, while urban youth had to try harder. However, the only criteria were to leave all inhibitions and pretense and learn the real technique to converse with a wide range of people from different economic and social structures.

Once the idea was clear to the representatives that there is no pressure to sell something, lose a job, or time constraint, they become natural friends. The environment at the service center where open discussion and camaraderie were encouraged, the whole personality change was observed.

AI and Customer Service

The team of IT professionals who were working on the AI development as a network startup under the IT Services cooperative company, which was established in the city of Vishram and extending throughout the country, had built a system with a huge database it could access. The customer service bots would work side by side with the Customer Service Reps and were implemented in the city as the first AI implementation in customer service to relieve Customer Service Reps of mundane tasks. Customer Service Reps needed to handle only the last interaction, and the whole system was so seamless that the local residents felt very comfortable knowing that their problem was solved with compassion and in a timely manner. It was noted that having only an AI or human representative would be a frustrating experience. The first experiment with the AI and customer service representative was a great success.

Sector-specific expert support

The other two sectors they could choose, other than support services, were a great initiative by Atif. Many interns changed their sectors several times before they were convinced that for a few years, they would work in those 2 sectors even though they were poles apart. But that is the beauty of Peopleism, giving workers choices based on their passion. Since most of the regular tasks are done by AI and technology, the workers were free to follow their passion and still get paid well.

To Atif's surprise, many of the interns chose healthcare as one of their sectors. One of the reasons cited by the interns was that they were still skeptical, and healthcare would be one area which would have work for a long time. "We can't blame them for being skeptical," said Sarah when they were discussing the progress of the internship. "It takes time," said Sarah.

Government and utilities customer service contract given to customer service representatives

Six months into the internship program, Atif and Sarah were a little nervous about getting the customer service work which could help the interns to start working on real projects and get paid. Even though the city and state government were paying the intern Customer Service Reps and IT Service Professionals internship, and they were paying it for one year. These internships would be finished in six months, and they would be working on real projects after completing the one year. The government officials were paying a visit to the facility and seeing the progress. Atif had many of the interactions with the local resident customers videotaped, and phone interactions with customer service bots were recorded. This impressed the government officials, and seeing the progress, had given the first contract to provide customer support for all the government services. By the end of the first year, Atif and Sarah managed to get all utility companies in the city of

Vishram to give a contract for customer service to Customer Service Reps as the sole customer service providers.

Empowering Local Resident Associations

Customer Service Reps in the last 3 months of their internship had created the resident network with all 5 regional communities. The Customer Service Reps helped the local resident communities to form resident associations and facilitated complaints, monthly meetings of residents with the city municipality officials, utility companies, and public works department to solve their problems. It was an amazing blend of excellent customer service, AI helping in monitoring the complaints, and Customer Service Reps following up with interaction with the residents. The residents of Vishram saw firsthand what customer service is.

The heart of Peopleism's success in Vishram was the transformation of customer service through the Customer Service Reps, the city's newly trained service representatives. These workers were more than just employees—they became genuine friends to the people, embodying compassion and understanding in their daily roles. Connecting with the residents was not just a task; it was the foundation of their new role, and through it, they transformed from ordinary workers into Customer Service Reps, or "friends of the people."

Each Customer Service Rep learned to engage with residents in person, over the phone, or even by visiting their homes—without the constraints of time, sales pressure, or quotas. This gave them the freedom to focus on truly helping others, building relationships that transcended the typical customer service experience.

The training process was rigorous, lasting three months. The trainees were taught to communicate effectively with residents from all walks of life. Surprisingly, many rural youths adapted to this new model of service faster than their urban counterparts, who found it harder to shed the competitive, corporate mentality. However, the key to success was leaving behind all pretenses and engaging with people authentically.

Among the trainees was Shereen, a fiery 22-year-old from a small village outside Vishram. She had never thought customer service could be something more than a routine job. "Back home, we treat everyone like family," she said during a training session. "Here, I'm learning to treat even strangers that way." Shereen's natural ability to connect with people quickly made her a standout, and she became a mentor to her fellow trainees, encouraging them to embrace their roles as more than just service providers.

In contrast, there was Ajay, an urban youth from Vishram itself, who initially struggled with the new approach. Used to the fast pace and transactional nature of city life, Ajay found it difficult to slow down and build genuine relationships. "At first, I did not get it," Ajay admitted. "But then I realized this is not about selling or meeting targets. It is about understanding people's problems and helping them—not for profit, but because it is the right thing to do." Ajay's transformation was slow but steady, and by the end of the program, he had become one of the most empathetic Customer Service Reps in his cohort.

Once the trainees grasped the idea that there was no pressure to sell or rush, they blossomed into natural community leaders. The environment at the service centers encouraged open discussions and camaraderie, creating a space where personal growth flourished. The change in personality was remarkable; they were not just workers anymore—they were friends of the people.

AI and Customer Service

Meanwhile, the city's AI integration project was moving full steam ahead. The IT Services Cooperative company, established in Vishram by a team of visionary technologists, developed an AI system to assist the Customer Service Reps. This system worked seamlessly alongside the human representatives, handling routine queries and tasks while allowing Customer Service Reps to focus on more complex, personal interactions. With access to a vast database, the AI bots efficiently managed the mundane, freeing up the Customer Service Reps to handle the final interaction, ensuring that residents' problems were solved with both speed and compassion.

Shereen found the collaboration with AI to be a game-changer. "The AI takes care of the boring stuff," she laughed during one shift. "It lets me focus on the person, not the process." Ajay, on the other hand, was initially skeptical. "I thought AI would take over my job," he admitted. "But it turns out, it's like a teammate—doing the heavy lifting so I can be more human."

The seamless integration of AI and human interaction led to a highly successful system. Residents felt their issues were being handled with care, and the customer service representatives, backed by AI support, had more time to invest in meaningful connections.

Sector-Specific Expert Support

Another innovative feature of Peopleism was the ability for Customer Service Reps to choose two additional sectors to explore beyond customer service. The flexibility to switch between sectors meant that these workers could follow their passions without fear of job instability. Many of the trainees switched between sectors several times before settling on their choices.

Shereen, always curious and eager to help, initially chose healthcare as her second sector. "I want to be where the people need us most," she explained. She found herself drawn to the human element of healthcare, knowing that it would allow her to continue serving the community in a meaningful way. Ajay, after much contemplation, decided to explore education. "I never thought I would want to teach, but after this experience, I realize I want to help others grow," he said.

This freedom to explore their interests, while still maintaining a steady income, was a defining feature of Peopleism. Even though most tasks were handled by AI and automation, workers were encouraged to follow their passions, knowing that their contributions were valued.

A Year of Success

As the first year of the program came to an end, Atif and Sarah reflected on how far they had come. "What a year," Atif said with a grin. "Our small project has grown wings, and now cities across the state are curious about what we've done." Sarah nodded, adding, "And we have only just begun. There are still so many sectors to explore. The future is going to be fascinating."

Together, they had laid the foundation for a new way of working and living—a future where technology and compassion went hand in hand, and where Vishram stood as a shining example of Peopleism's promise.

Second Year for IT Professionals, Management Professionals, and customer service representatives

In the bustling city of Vishram, a transformative internship was underway for IT professionals and Customer Service Reps, customer service trainees. By the time they reached the halfway point of their first year, the IT professionals were mastering technology and AI tools, while the Customer Service Reps were determining their career specializations. It was not just about honing skills; it was about using technology to solve real-world problems from the consumer's perspective. This involved integrating various AI-powered solutions into one cohesive system, designed to serve the people of Vishram.

Building Sector-Specific AI Assistants

Atif was committed to a solution where technology would work for everyone, not just a few corporations. He believed in developing sector-specific AI Agents—digital assistants that would handle transportation needs from a consumer perspective. But his vision was not limited to technology alone; he saw it as part of a larger economic model where service providers, IT professionals, management professionals, and customer service agents worked together in a collaborative ecosystem.

"Technology should be owned by the people who build it," Atif asserted during a meeting with the IT interns. "We need to cap the profits technology companies can make. IT professionals should earn a fair 5% royalty for developing solutions, and customer service providers like the Customer Service Reps should get 10% for providing support services for consumers, and Management professionals should make 5% for the organizations and sector-specific companies to manage professionally using technology. The remaining 80% of the revenue should go to the service providers in different sectors. This is the Peopleism model."

The service providers using AI tools and AI agents, supported by customer service representatives, would provide efficient services for the consumers.

The Transportation Crisis in Vishram

In Vishram, traffic was a nightmare. Roads were constantly jammed, and public transportation was overcrowded and unreliable, turning commutes into an exhausting ordeal. Frustrated with the delays and discomfort, more residents leaned on rideshare services or their own vehicles, hoping for a reprieve. But instead of solving the problem, this reliance on private vehicles only worsened the congestion, pollution, and travel times. The gig economy grew, drawing young people from rural areas to Vishram as drivers, but the lack of coordination left the city's infrastructure crumbling.

Atif saw that the solution required more than another app or startup. Unlike traditional models where companies handled everything from technology to logistics, he proposed a Network Startup model with cooperatives managing different aspects of the solution.

"Develop the technology and AI agents to solve the issues," Atif told his team, "but your responsibility is to maintain and upgrade the tech. You will earn royalties from the usage—5% of the service fee. That way, you're free from managing the entire business."

One intern, Matt, looked confused. "So we just build the tech, and that is it? We're not managing drivers or customer service?"

"Exactly," Atif said. "Look at rideshare apps. They all offer nearly the same service with identical pricing, yet they compete fiercely. It is inefficient. Our model lets IT experts develop the tech, Customer Service Reps handle customer support, and the bulk of earnings goes to service providers—drivers and public transport managers. Everyone wins."

Transforming the Commute

Roshni, an IT consultant commuting two hours daily, was one of the first to try Atif's AI-powered Commuter Assistant. After years of canceled rides and long waits, she was forced to buy her own car, while her husband still used ride-shares due to his shorter commute. But with the pilot program, Roshni was ready to give public transport another shot.

The Commuter Assistant offered dynamic, real-time routing, combining various modes—rideshare, metro, carpool—to find the fastest, most affordable path. On her first day, Roshni's commute involved a shared rickshaw, a metro ride, and carpooling. The AI smoothly guided her, prompting her to switch modes at the right times.

Drivers, too, saw improvements. The app's AI guided them through efficient pickups and routes in their language, coordinating with public transport so that common points became routine, reducing the frustrations of waiting and unpredictable stops.

Public transportation began operating in sync with commuter schedules, with AI managing capacity to prevent overcrowding. Casual travelers faced a surcharge for unscheduled trips, encouraging them to plan ahead. Soon, even occasional travelers saw the benefits of pre-scheduling, making Vishram's transport network more predictable for everyone.

At first, there were a few hiccups in switching between modes, but soon the app was running flawlessly. Roshni completed her commute stress-free, and within six months, thousands in Vishram were using the app. Whether switching from a scooter to the metro or sharing a rickshaw, the AI made commutes smoother, faster, and easier to navigate.

A Citywide Shift

The AI-powered Commuter Assistant transformed Vishram overnight. Streets cleared as more residents embraced ridesharing and public transport, each routed by AI to the fastest, most efficient options. Commuters enjoyed quicker, predictable journeys, while drivers found less traffic and shorter wait times, making their workdays easier and more profitable.

For commuters, the app became a lifeline. No more missed buses or traffic jams. Real-time updates, traffic alerts, and route suggestions made daily travel seamless. The reduced car usage lowered pollution and shaved minutes off everyone's commutes, creating a ripple effect citywide.

Customer Service Reps, the human element, ensured that everything ran smoothly. Although AI handled coordination, Customer Service Reps were on hand to resolve issues—whether a roadblock or a miscommunication. Their presence reassured commuters that someone was there to help, bridging any gaps technology could not fill.

Drivers, too, felt the change. They faced less traffic, meaning more fares in less time. The AI optimized rides and reduced idle time, improving earnings and easing stress. What was once a chaotic, draining workday became efficient and manageable, enhancing their quality of life.

Behind it all, Atif's team continued refining the app. They gathered feedback from Customer Service Reps, commuters, and drivers to enhance the AI's performance. Managing millions of real-time commutes was no small feat, yet the AI processed it all to deliver accurate guidance.

Recognition and Reward for Innovators

Atif watched with pride as the app improved the lives of Vishram's residents. The Customer Service Reps' feedback campaign led to a citywide celebration of the IT team's work. At a public ceremony, the team received heartfelt thanks, not just from commuters but from the whole city.

For the IT professionals, many of whom had come from major tech companies, the recognition was unlike anything they had experienced. In a typical corporate setting, their work would have been lost amid profits flowing up to shareholders. But in Vishram, under Peopleism, their contributions were rewarded directly.

Through a 5% royalty on the app's usage, the developers earned ongoing income beyond the initial development. This financial stability allowed them to focus on passion projects without the usual corporate pressure. As the app expanded to other cities, their earnings grew, providing a stable, fulfilling livelihood.

In a capitalist model, profits from such an app would have gone to big tech companies. But here, those who built the app reaped the benefits. The commuter assistant was not just a tech success—it was proof of Peopleism's power, showing how innovation could benefit all who contributed to it.

A Model for Change

Sarah, following the pilot project, was thrilled with the results. To her, the transportation model was a Peopleism blueprint that could transform other sectors. "This is a win for Peopleism, Atif," she said during a seminar where Roshni shared her experiences. "We used technology to solve a real problem without displacing workers. Everyone—the IT professionals, Customer Service Reps, service providers—benefited equally. It's a model we can apply city by city, sector by sector."

Atif nodded, reflecting on their journey. What began as an internship project had grown into a city-changing solution. And as he looked forward, he saw the potential for this approach to revolutionize industries everywhere, using technology to empower rather than replace people.

Healthcare for All in Vishram: A Journey Toward Compassionate, Accessible Healthcare

Sarah sat in her office, staring at the thick report in front of her, but her mind was elsewhere. The walls of her modest workspace seemed to close in around her as she absorbed the weight of the document in her hands. This was not just a collection of numbers or statistics; this report, compiled by Dr. Shafi and Dr. Rehana, told the story of a healthcare system that had failed its people. It was a story of human suffering, of families bankrupted by hospital bills, and of lives lost due to corruption and inefficiency.

Sarah had asked these two trusted doctors to help her investigate the healthcare situation in Vishram, her home city. She wanted to see it through their eyes—through the lens of professionals who had spent their lives on the front lines of patient care. What they found was worse than she had imagined.

As she read, memories of recent conversations flooded back. Just days earlier, Dr. Shafi had sat in her office, shaking his head. "The system is bleeding people dry, Sarah," he had said, his voice thick with frustration. "Patients come in for a simple fever and walk out with debts they will never pay off. And for what? Tests they did not need, drugs they did not want, and procedures they never should have had."

His words still hung in the air. The private hospitals, funded by Wall Street investors, operated like profit-driven machines. Doctors were no longer salaried employees dedicated to patient care; they were consultants, bouncing from one hospital to another, racking up commissions from pharmaceutical companies and laboratories for every test they ordered and every drug they prescribed. The cycle of greed was endless.

Sarah could still hear the sorrow in Dr. Rehana's voice as she recounted the story of a young man fresh out of college. "He came in with a fever," she had said. "It should have been a quick visit—a diagnosis, a prescription, and then home. But instead, they kept him overnight for 'observation.' They ran test after test, none of them necessary, and when it was all over, his family was left with a bill they could not pay." Rehana had sighed deeply. "It is unethical. But it is also the reality we live in."

Sarah closed her eyes, trying to imagine the young man's family, bewildered and overwhelmed by the maze of invoices, baffled by the charges for treatments they had not even known were happening. And yet, this was not an isolated case—this was happening across the city.

Even outside the walls of private hospitals, the public system offered little hope. Sarah had seen it firsthand during a visit to a local market. She had stopped at a small shop to speak with the owner, a middle-aged man with tired eyes and a voice that cracked with exhaustion. "We pray we do not get sick," he had told her. "Because once you step into a hospital—public or private—it is over. The hospital, the tests, the medicines… they will take everything you have."

His words had cut through Sarah like a knife. He was right. The public hospitals were no sanctuary. Though treatment was theoretically free, they were overcrowded and starved of resources. Patients had to bribe their way to the front of lines or wait months for critical procedures. Sarah had heard stories of families selling their homes just to afford under-the-table payments that sped up their loved ones' care. The cashier at a local grocery store had quietly confessed how she had slipped money to hospital staff so her mother could receive urgent treatment. "There's no empathy," she had said. "It's every man for himself."

Sarah's heart ached for these people—people who deserved better. She could not shake the feeling that the system had forgotten them, leaving them trapped in a cycle of exploitation. But amidst this sea of suffering, Sarah saw a glimmer of hope. Dr. Shafi and Dr. Rehana were not just disillusioned by the system—they were determined to change it. Dr. Shafi had even started a small telemedicine project to bring healthcare to rural areas, though he was the first to admit it was merely a band-aid on a much larger wound.

Sarah, too, was committed to change. She had always believed that healthcare was a basic human right, and the situation in Vishram only strengthened her resolve. She knew what had to be done. They had just trained and provided an internship to the support personnel Customer Service Reps— the group of local community health workers trained to assist with healthcare delivery—Sarah was ready to embark on a bold journey to transform healthcare in Vishram.

The Four-Step Plan for Transforming Healthcare

Sarah's vision was not just a lofty ideal—it was grounded in a concrete, four-step plan that would reshape healthcare in Vishram from the ground up. Her solution was inspired by the principles of Peopleism, an economic philosophy she believed in deeply, where the well-being of people would be prioritized over profit.

Step 1: AI-Powered Healthcare Assistant

The first step in the transformation was to harness the power of technology to support healthcare workers. Sarah's plan centered around developing an

AI-powered healthcare assistant that could streamline the diagnostic and treatment process, giving doctors the tools they needed to make informed decisions quickly and accurately.

Dr. Shafi, ever the optimist when it came to innovation, was thrilled by the prospect. "We are always drowning in paperwork," he had said after one of the first test runs of the AI system. "If this works, we can actually spend time with our patients again—talk to them, listen to them, instead of just filling out forms."

The AI system would analyze diagnostic results, offer insights into drug interactions, and monitor patient recovery—all in real-time. Doctors would not have to rely on endless tests to figure out what was wrong. Instead, the AI could provide a list of likely diagnoses, allowing doctors to focus on patient care rather than paperwork.

It was not just about making healthcare more efficient, though. For Sarah, it was about restoring the humanity that had been lost in the quest for profit. "The AI is not here to replace doctors," she often told skeptics. "It's here to help them make better decisions for their patients."

Step 2: Community-Owned Captive Insurance

Next, Sarah knew that the system could not be funded by traditional means. The second step in her plan was to create a community-owned captive insurance company. Sarah had learned about captive insurance models in Western countries, where large corporations created their own insurance pools to cover employee healthcare. But in Vishram, this insurance company would be owned by the people.

The funds would come from a combination of sources: contributions from employee insurance programs, government subsidies for those below the poverty line, and premiums paid by the general population. But the key difference was that the insurance company would be managed by the residents of Vishram themselves.

This way, there would be no profit-hungry middlemen. Every rupee collected would be used to pay for healthcare services, not to line the pockets of private insurers. "If we control the money," Sarah said, "we can control the care."

Step 3: Empowering customer service representatives

The third step focused on the Customer Service Reps, a crucial part of the healthcare system in Vishram. These community health workers were more than just administrative assistants – they were the heart of the city's wellness program. Sarah had always believed in the power of community support, and the Customer Service Reps would play a central role in making sure that no patient slipped through the cracks.

Sarah allocated 10% of the healthcare system's budget to fund the Customer Service Reps, ensuring they were fairly compensated for their work. They were not just there to schedule appointments or file paperwork. Customer Service Reps would visit patients in their homes, check on their progress, and offer support for preventive care measures. In rural areas, where healthcare was often inaccessible, the Customer Service Reps were an essential lifeline.

With the AI system backing them, the Customer Service Reps could provide personalized care to every patient in the city, ensuring that the healthcare system was not just reactive, but proactive.

Step 4: Healthcare Provider Cooperatives

The final step was perhaps the most revolutionary. Sarah proposed that healthcare providers themselves—doctors, nurses, technicians—form their own cooperative company managed by management professionals, and IT professionals would provide the required AI and technology. Instead of being employed by profit-driven hospitals or corporate chains, they would be shareholders of their own healthcare facilities.

This would remove the incentive for doctors to perform unnecessary tests or prescribe overpriced medicines. With no shareholders to answer to, they could focus entirely on patient care. The cooperative model would foster a sense of collaboration, not competition, among healthcare professionals.

Sarah envisioned a future where doctors worked for the well-being of their patients, not for the bottom line. By owning their own clinics and hospitals, healthcare workers would have the autonomy they needed to practice ethically, and they would be paid fairly for their work.

A New Dawn for Healthcare

The road to transformation was not easy, but it was worth it. As Sarah, Atif, and their team began to implement the four-step plan, the healthcare landscape in Vishram started to change. The AI-powered healthcare assistant allowed doctors to spend more time with their patients. The Customer Service Reps became trusted figures in every neighborhood, offering support and guidance. And most importantly, the community-owned insurance model gave the people of Vishram control over their own healthcare.

Dr. Shafi and Dr. Rehana remained at the forefront, guiding the project and ensuring that the system stayed true to its values of compassion, fairness and accessibility.

The long lines at government hospitals grew shorter, and the fear of hospital bills faded away. In its place was a system that worked for everyone – a system that put people first.

Sarah's dream of healthcare for all had become a reality in Vishram. And as word spread of the success, other cities began to take notice. Vishram had become a beacon of hope, a living example of what was possible when healthcare was built on the principles of compassion and cooperation.

Education in the City of Vishram: A Journey Toward Transformation

Sarah and Atif sat in the brightly lit meeting room, the afternoon sun casting long shadows across the floor. The energy in the room was palpable as Reshma, a social worker and passionate advocate for education, laid out the dire state of the city of Vishram's schooling system. "If you want to understand what's happening in education here, you need to see the government school in Sector 4," she urged. "The principal there, John Bernard, has been fighting to keep that school running against all odds."

Sarah, ever the realist, and Atif, a visionary with experience in education reform, exchanged a glance. They knew they could not rely on reports alone – they needed to see it for themselves.

The next morning, they arrived at the government school in Sector 4 just as the lunch break began. The scene was one of stark contrast—children playing with a deflated football on a dusty playground while the large school building stood in the background, its faded walls a testament to years of neglect. They were greeted by Principal Bernard, a tall, soft-spoken man whose deep lines of exhaustion were offset by a glimmer of hope in his eyes.

"This school was the pride of the community," Bernard began as he led them through the building. "It was the first one built in this area, and we used to have resources—sports equipment, science labs, art classes. But now, we are barely managing with what we have." He gestured toward a classroom where children sat at broken desks, some staring out of the window while others were glued to their textbooks. "Many of these kids come here just for the midday meal. For some, it is the only proper meal they will get all day."

Sarah's heart sank as she observed the worn-out faces of the students. The atmosphere reminded her of other underfunded schools she had visited in similar areas, where survival often overshadowed education.

"I have been applying for government funding for years," Bernard continued, frustration evident in his voice. "But every time, it is the same story. The funds either do not arrive, or they are not enough to make any real difference. We need educational tools, technology, and support if we are going to prepare these kids for the world outside."

Atif, who had been quietly taking it all in, finally spoke. "The school has so much potential. There's space here, resources could be brought in, but why hasn't the government invested in rebuilding the infrastructure?"

Bernard's shoulders sagged as he responded. "Most of the funding we get goes to basic maintenance. It is not just this school; every government school in Vishram is struggling. Meanwhile, private schools are springing up everywhere, luring parents with promises of better facilities and exam scores. But these private schools—" he paused, shaking his head, "—they are businesses, not places of learning."

The conversation shifted to the proliferation of private schools in Vishram. Sarah and Atif had seen them everywhere—flashy advertisements plastered on billboards, promising top exam results and the latest educational technologies. But the reality behind the glossy ads was far from ideal.

"Private schools in Vishram have become money-making machines," Reshma chimed in, her frustration evident. "It is not about educating children anymore. It is about getting them to pass exams and move on. The students are not learning how to think—they are just memorizing information. And the worst part? Parents are falling for it because they think paying more means better education."

Atif agreed, recalling the successes of public schools in the U.S., where his children had studied. "In the U.S., public education is free, accessible, and backed by government funding. Students have access to transportation, infrastructure, and skilled teachers. We could learn from that system, but here in Vishram, the situation is much more complicated."

Sarah, however, knew that the issue ran deeper than just money. "It is not just about copying another system," she said thoughtfully. "The problem is political. The government is cutting funding for public schools to push more children into private institutions. It is all about profit, not education."

As Sarah and Atif reflected on their visit to Sector 4, they knew that simply pumping more money into the current system was not the answer. Something deeper had to change. That is when Reshma suggested a bold new approach: integrating AI into the education system and shifting the focus to a Montessori-based model for younger children.

"We need to stop forcing children to sit in classrooms and memorize facts," Reshma explained. "The Montessori system allows children to explore their natural interests, and AI can help each child learn at their own pace."

Atif was immediately intrigued. Having worked in the tech industry, he knew the potential of AI. "With AI tools, students do not need to rely solely on a teacher lecturing in front of the room," he said. "Each student can have a personalized learning experience, using AI to assist them with subjects they find difficult and to push them further in areas where they excel."

The idea began to take shape: a hybrid system that combined Montessori principles for young learners and AI-powered educational tools for older students. With this system, students would no longer be limited by outdated syllabi or overworked teachers. Instead, they would be free to explore their interests and learn at a pace that suited them.

Over the next few weeks, Sarah, Atif, and Reshma worked closely with Principal Bernard and a group of dedicated parents to introduce the idea of AI and Montessori-based education to the community. At first, there was resistance. Parents were skeptical. "We didn't grow up with AI," one parent said during a meeting. "How can we trust a machine to teach our kids?"

But Reshma had a way with words. She gently reminded the parents that the world was changing, and the traditional education system no longer prepared children for the future. "We're not teaching our children how to live in the world we grew up in," she said. "We're preparing them for a world that's evolving rapidly. AI is going to be a part of that world, whether we like it or not. And by integrating it into their education, we're giving them a head start."

Slowly, the parents began to come around. They saw how the Montessori system could give their children more freedom to learn in ways that suited them. They also saw the benefits of AI in leveling the playing field—no child would be left behind because the teacher could not give them enough attention.

As the new educational system was rolled out in Vishram, the changes were immediate and profound. Teachers, once burdened by large class sizes and outdated materials, found themselves relieved by the integration of AI tools. "I no longer have to spend hours grading papers or struggling to reach every student," one teacher said. "AI handles the basics, and I can focus on actually teaching."

The students were thriving too. With AI-based learning platforms, each student progressed at their own pace. Those who excelled in certain subjects could advance without being held back, while those who needed extra help received it through personalized lessons. Students explored subjects they were passionate about—whether it was learning multiple languages, diving into robotics, or exploring new creative outlets.

The rigid structures of the past were gone. College study was no longer confined to a single subject. Students graduated with degrees that not only reflected their major field of study but also included other subjects they had pursued as hobbies or interests. Even medical education evolved. Aspiring doctors learned technology alongside empathy and compassion, ensuring that the future of healthcare was driven by both AI and human understanding.

Sarah and Atif had become catalysts for transformation in Vishram. The educational landscape was changing, and the shift was not just about using AI or adopting a new teaching model—it was about embracing the future. The children of Vishram were no longer preparing for a world that no longer existed. They were preparing for the world of tomorrow, a world where AI, technology, and creativity would guide them forward.

What started as a visit to an underfunded school in Sector 4 sparked a revolution. Education, once stagnant and burdened by politics and profit, was now free, accessible, and powered by the latest technology. The people of Vishram had embraced a new way of thinking, and as education and healthcare improved, they began to realize that Peopleism—an economic model where everyone had a stake in the future—was becoming a reality in their lives.

Sarah smiled as she watched the children of Vishram running across the playground, their laughter filling the air. She and Atif had played a part in something much bigger than themselves, something that would shape the future for generations to come. The journey toward transformation had only just begun.

Food Security in Vishram: A Peopleism Solution

The city of Vishram, once surrounded by fertile farmlands, had long relied on local farms for its supply of vegetables, chicken, and mutton. These farms had formed a cooperative that supplied fresh produce to outlets across the city, ensuring a stable income for the farmers. However, over the years, urban expansion encroached on the rural areas, and many farmers sold their land to real estate developers, leaving behind dwindling agricultural operations. The remaining farmers struggled with unpredictable weather patterns—droughts, floods, and erratic rainfall—leading to a significant decline in local food production. The city began sourcing much of its food from distant regions, increasing both costs and food waste.

Recognizing the crisis, Atif and Sarah decided that food security would be a key focus of the second year of Peopleism's implementation in Vishram. The challenges were mounting: nearly 60% of perishable food now came from sources 400 to 500 kilometers away, and about 30% of that food was wasted before it even reached consumers. Moreover, during natural disasters, up to 70% of cultivated food could be lost. With thousands of hungry people in Vishram, this wastage was nothing short of criminal.

Local Solutions for Food Security

Dr. Gracy, a professor of agricultural economics at the local university, had been researching the food security issues in Vishram for years. A firm believer in local economic development, she reached out to Sarah with a comprehensive report on the topic. When they met, Dr. Gracy laid out the alarming statistics and issues. "The deterioration of local farms has been catastrophic," she explained. "The cooperative system that once ensured fresh produce reached the city by 6 a.m. daily has crumbled. Farmers used to receive a minimum support price that covered their costs plus a 50% profit, but now they are at the mercy of auctions. If a particular vegetable is abundant that day, prices plummet, and the farmers often do not even recoup their costs."

Dr. Gracy continued, "What is worse is that while farmers suffer, consumers still pay inflated prices due to inefficiencies and middlemen. Vegetables pass through several hands before they reach the city's outlets, adding to both cost and waste."

A New Vision: Vertical Farming and the Revival of the Cooperative

Atif listened intently and then spoke up, "We have the technology now to change this. But what is your solution?"

Dr. Gracy was prepared. She proposed a system of vertical farming, greenhouses, and controlled environments to mitigate the effects of climate change. She also suggested that the remaining rural land around Vishram could be revitalized to restore production to what it was a decade ago. "If we re-establish the cooperative and implement professional management, farmers could once again earn a good income while ensuring a stable food supply for the city," she explained.

Sarah, inspired by the plan, added, "The cooperative needs to be professionally managed by experts, with full support from customer service representatives. We can start by creating a network of farmers and farm workers to assess the current production and understand the challenges they face. We should also involve the local vendors who sell the produce in the city."

Expanding Beyond Raw Produce: The Role of Self-Help Groups (SHGs)

Dr. Gracy then expanded her vision. "Food security is not just about raw produce. Many people in Vishram either do not have the time to cook or cannot afford restaurant food. While food delivery seems popular, it is a misconception—only about 10% of the population can afford to order regularly. For the majority, cooking at home or eating street food, which may be unsafe or unhygienic, are their only options."

Atif was surprised. "Looking at all the delivery workers, it seemed like a booming industry. So, what is your solution?"

Dr. Gracy explained that re-establishing the farmers' cooperative was only the first step. The outlets around the city should be owned and operated by Self-Help Groups (SHGs), composed primarily of women engaged in low-wage jobs. These SHGs would not only sell or deliver vegetables, fruits, and meat but also operate cloud kitchens in each neighborhood. They would prepare healthy, affordable meals and deliver them to consumers locally.

"The SHGs can secure low-interest loans from banks to buy produce directly from the farmers," Dr. Gracy said. "They would manage both the sale of raw food and the operation of the cloud kitchens, ensuring food is accessible to everyone, not just the wealthy."

Sarah was impressed. "This is a brilliant solution! We can pilot this program in one area and expand it gradually."

The Role of Technology: AI-Driven Food Distribution

Atif, excited by the possibilities, offered his expertise. "We can provide the necessary technology with AI-powered apps to streamline the process. Consumers can order food through an app, and we can use local hawkers for delivery. There's no need to involve highly educated workers—Customer Service Reps can manage customer service and handle the logistics."

The team decided to launch the pilot program in Sector 4 of Vishram. SHG women took charge of the cooperative, the cloud kitchens, and the delivery system. Farmers were finally receiving fair prices for their produce, while consumers enjoyed reduced costs on fresh fruits, vegetables, and healthy cooked meals. The cloud kitchens, equipped with modern amenities, delivered fresh food within minutes, ensuring quality and convenience.

A Success Story: Scaling Across Vishram and Beyond

The pilot was a resounding success. The SHG women, farmers, hawkers, and consumers all embraced the new system. The price of produce fell, but farmers were earning more than ever before. The cloud kitchens provided nutritious, hygienic meals at affordable prices, catering to a wide range of people who previously had few options for healthy food.

Dr. Gracy and her team quickly took responsibility for expanding the initiative to other parts of Vishram. Atif, seeing the potential of the model, packaged it as a replicable solution and invited teams from across the country – and even internationally – to implement it in their own cities.

The Peopleism model, with its focus on cooperative ownership, technology-driven efficiency, and community-based solutions, had not only addressed Vishram's food security crisis but also created a sustainable, inclusive food system that could serve as a blueprint for cities around the world.

The Future of Peopleism

The success of Vishram's transportation, resident services, healthcare, food security, and education solutions marked just the beginning of the second year for the IT professionals and Customer Service Reps. With transportation in Vishram under control, the team was already looking to apply the same principles to other sectors. The AI assistants would not be confined to solving traffic problems – they could be adapted to manage patient care, streamline educational pathways, and coordinate community services.

For now, though, the city of Vishram stood as a shining example of what could be achieved when technology, customer service, and human ingenuity came together in the spirit of Peopleism. With AI as the engine and people as the drivers, the future looked brighter than ever.

* * *

Chapter 13

THE CASE FOR PEOPLEISM IN INDIA

After seeing Peopleism thrive in Vishram, Sarah and Atif were inspired. The results were beyond anything they had hoped for, proving that Peopleism is not just an economic model—it is a movement for change. Now, Sarah was pouring all her findings into a report that would make the case for implementing Peopleism across India. "This report doesn't just explain the 'why'," she told Atif, handing him a draft, "it maps out exactly 'how' Peopleism can uplift India—nationwide."

Atif skimmed the report, his eyes lighting up. "This is exactly what India needs," he said. "Our economy's rapid growth is leaving millions behind, while the top 1% amass most of the new wealth. Peopleism doesn't just offer a solution; it aligns with our Constitution's call for economic and social justice."

Sarah smiled. "Exactly. Peopleism is not a new idea—it is rooted in the Constitution, specifically Article 39, which envisions an India where resources are used for the common good and wealth is shared equitably. Dr. Ambedkar foresaw these challenges. He knew we would need an economic model that puts people, not profits, at the center."

The Need for Peopleism: Key Findings from the Report

1. **Growing Inequality:** Despite impressive economic growth, India's wealth is concentrated in the hands of a few, with the top 1% capturing 73% of the nation's newly created wealth each year. The result? Millions live in poverty, while half the population depends on government food handouts. Peopleism seeks to address this by redistributing wealth generated from technology, infrastructure, and natural resources, aligning with Article 39's vision of equitable resource distribution.

2. **Technological Displacement of Jobs:** Automation and AI are transforming industries but displacing jobs. Many young Indians face an uncertain future, juggling gig work without benefits or security. Peopleism proposes a system where AI-driven profits are not funneled to corporations alone but distributed across worker-owned cooperatives, empowering everyone to benefit from technological advancement.

3. **Harnessing the Demographic Dividend:** With over 900 million Indians under 35, India holds the potential for an economic "demographic dividend." However, without fair opportunities and wealth distribution, this potential could lead to a demographic disaster. Peopleism addresses this by creating a system where every young person has a chance to thrive, in line with the Constitution's promise of economic justice.

4. **Wealth Creation Without Labor:** By 2028, technology will drive 60% of India's wealth creation, but much of this wealth is locked up with corporations and elites. Peopleism argues that this wealth should be distributed more broadly, allowing all citizens to benefit from technological progress—a principle the Constitution already supports by aiming to prevent wealth concentration in the hands of a few.

How Peopleism Aligns with the Indian Constitution

Sarah looked at Atif. "Here's where it gets fascinating. Peopleism isn't just compatible with our Constitution—it brings its values to life."

"Let's look at some of the key principles," she continued, referencing the pages in her report.

- **Right to Livelihood (Article 39(a))** "When we talk about livelihood, we are talking about income, not just jobs," Sarah explained. "Dr. Ambedkar knew jobs might not be the only source of income in the future." Peopleism provides citizens with a share of the wealth generated by AI and natural resources, creating new income streams that supplement traditional wages.

- **Equitable Resource Distribution (Article 39(b))** Peopleism mandates those profits from resources—like minerals, technology, and infrastructure—benefit all citizens, not just a privileged few. This aligns with the constitutional vision of using resources for the common good.

- **Preventing Wealth Concentration (Article 39(c))**Through worker cooperatives, Peopleism addresses wealth concentration directly. "Profits don't just go to CEOs and shareholders," Sarah said, "they go to the people who do the work."

- **Universal Healthcare and Education (Articles 39(d) and (e))** Peopleism extends the right to free, universal healthcare and education, ensuring that these fundamental needs are met for everyone. Under this model, healthcare and education become rights, not privileges, fulfilling the Constitution's call for economic and social justice.

Reclaiming the Workforce: A Right to Livelihood for Every Worker

India's workforce numbers approximately 600 million, with many trapped in low-wage, unorganized sectors. Only 13% have permanent jobs with benefits. In Peopleism, all working-age individuals would be members of cooperative companies, sharing in profits and earning dividends as shareholders. No longer just employees, they would be co-owners with a vested interest in their industry's success.

"We are talking about a real transformation," Sarah said. "Imagine an India where a factory worker or an IT professional is both an employee and a shareholder. Every worker shares in the wealth they help create."

Wealth Creation Without Labor: Technology for All

Today, 65% of India's wealth is created by technology-driven sectors like IT and finance, often without human labor. In Peopleism, these profits would not just enrich corporations – they would be shared with the people, creating a baseline income for everyone. Workers in traditional sectors, like agriculture, would no longer be left behind, ensuring the Constitution's vision of fairness.

Cooperatives and Sector-Based Income Distribution: A Path to Shared Wealth

Peopleism proposes sector-based cooperative companies, where workers, not distant executives, own and run the businesses. By capping fees for support services, Peopleism ensures more revenue is shared among worker-owners. "In a Peopleist economy," Sarah explained, "no one is left out. Everyone has a stake in the economy, whether they work in agriculture or AI."

Leveraging IT and AI to Anchor a New Economy

India's tech sector could power this transformation, with IT professionals guiding cooperative companies toward digital solutions. Peopleism caps service fees, ensuring cooperatives retain more profit while benefiting from professional support. "This model brings professional management to the people," Sarah noted, "avoiding the pitfalls of past public-sector inefficiencies."

Ownership, Control and Distribution of Resources: Returning Wealth to the People

- **Article 39(b)** calls for resources to be managed for the common good, not corporate gain. Peopleism's vision puts resources—coal, minerals, technology—under collective ownership, allowing communities to control their wealth.

- **Article 39(c)** aims to prevent wealth from pooling at the top. Peopleism achieves this through worker cooperatives, ensuring profits benefit everyone, not just executives.

Peopleism also addresses the mismanagement of resources, where India's natural wealth has historically benefited private corporations more than the public. With a cooperative management approach, Peopleism ensures that resources are processed domestically, creating jobs and higher profits.

Reversing Wealth Concentration: Powering the Economy through People Ownership

Peopleism prevents private monopolies from controlling essential infrastructure like telecommunications, transportation, and energy. Profits are redirected back to citizens, funding essential services and securing the Constitution's mandate for shared prosperity.

National Asset Management for Collective Wealth

To manage India's wealth, Peopleism proposes a Technology, Infrastructure, and Natural Resources Fund in the form of a national asset management company owned by people, channeling profits from these sectors back into society. Instead of enriching corporations, this fund invests in essential services, renewables, and national projects. "It's a system that guarantees every Indian a share of the wealth," Sarah explained, "transforming our economy from the ground up."

AI and Universal Healthcare: Revolutionizing Public Health

Peopleism's approach to healthcare ensures access for all by consolidating fragmented systems into one universal plan. AI-powered diagnostics extend healthcare to rural areas, making high-quality medical care affordable and accessible. Article 39(d) calls for this universal approach, ensuring all citizens can live healthy, productive lives.

Transforming Education: AI as a Teacher's Assistant

Under Peopleism, AI technology would support teachers, helping to personalize learning and ensure every child receives quality education. By funding education through national resource profits, Peopleism guarantees that education up to Grade 12 is free for all, reducing inequality and preparing India's youth for the future.

A Call for Action: Building India's Future Together

Sarah closed her report with a powerful message: "India stands at a crossroads. We can either follow a path where inequality worsens and opportunity fades, or we can adopt Peopleism and create a future of shared prosperity." With Vishram's success as proof, she and Atif believed Peopleism could transform India into a nation that values, uplifts, and includes every citizen.

This is the vision of Peopleism – a new economic dawn where the people of India are not just workers but owners, not just citizens but stakeholders, sharing in the nation's growth, wealth, and future.

* * *

Chapter 14

A NEW WORLD

Years later, Atif stood under the golden glow of the late afternoon sun, watching the ribbon-cutting ceremony of a Technology Services Center in a small, rural town. A light breeze rustled the leaves of nearby trees, carrying with it the scent of the earth and the quiet hum of contentment that seemed to blanket the area. It was a world away from the bustling city life he once knew, but in this moment, he felt more connected to the future than ever before.

The journey had been long, full of challenges, setbacks, and moments of doubt, but here he was, witnessing the culmination of a vision that had once seemed impossible. Technology, once feared for its power to divide, had now bridged the gap between the city and the countryside. The townspeople, many of whom had once considered leaving for the allure of the big city, now chose to stay. Sarah had been right all along— "Let's bring the city to the countryside," she would said with a knowing smile. And they had.

Atif remembered his own childhood, growing up in a rural village much like this one. Back then, the only path to success was to leave—to abandon the verdant fields, the simple lifestyle, and move to a crowded, chaotic city. The cities had beckoned with promises of opportunity but often left young people disillusioned, trapped in a cycle of grueling work and disconnected from their roots. Atif had been one of those who left, but today, as he stood in this town, surrounded by families, farmers, and young entrepreneurs, he realized how far they had come from those days.

Sarah stood beside him, her smile reflecting the warmth of the afternoon. Together, they had transformed this vision into reality. "We did it," she whispered, her eyes scanning the joyful faces around them. "We brought the future here."

They had toured the local school earlier that day. The classrooms were filled with children, their eager faces illuminated by the light from smartboards and interactive screens. Teachers guided them, but they were not alone—AI tools assisted in ways that Atif had once only dreamed of. The children were not just learning the basics; they were exploring topics that went far beyond their years, dabbling in foreign languages, coding, and advanced sciences. AI had freed teachers to focus on the creative and emotional development of the children, while the technology handled the more routine educational tasks. It was education reimagined, and the results spoke for themselves.

Atif marveled at the way the students, most of whom had never ventured beyond the borders of their town, could speak to children across the world through virtual classrooms. They were learning, growing, and thriving, not in spite of their rural surroundings, but because of them. For the first time in generations, staying in the countryside was not a resignation to a life of limitation; it was an opportunity to flourish.

That evening, as the sun dipped below the horizon, casting the landscape in shades of orange and purple, Atif and Sarah joined the villagers at the community center. The air was filled with laughter, and the rhythmic beat of folk drums echoed through the open space. Men, women, and children, all dressed in their traditional attire, danced in a circle, their feet moving in sync with the age-old rhythms passed down from their ancestors. But this was not just nostalgia for the past. The dances, the songs, the community— they had all been reinvigorated by the hope and prosperity of this new world. It was a celebration of who they were and what they had become.

The transformation extended far beyond education. The very lifeblood of rural life—farming—had undergone a revolution. The once unpredictable rains no longer determined the success or failure of crops. Vertical farming, powered by AI and automation, had taken root. Greenhouses dotted the landscape, their walls lined with shelves of produce growing in carefully controlled environments. Every drop of water was recycled, and every square inch of space was maximized. The old ways of farming, where waste and inefficiency ruled, were a distant memory. The new system ensured that fresh, local produce reached the nearby cities in record time, with AI handling the logistics to ensure seamless distribution. The supply chains, once riddled with waste and delay, were now optimized to near perfection.

"Can you believe it?" Atif mused to Sarah as they watched the villagers' dance. "The system's so efficient now that food reaches the cities faster from here than it used to from industrial farms."

Sarah nodded; her eyes gleaming with satisfaction. "It is more than just efficiency. It is sustainability. We are not just feeding people – we are nourishing them, body and soul."

She was right, of course. The farming system, like everything else in this new world, was not just about productivity; it was about balance, about finding a way to coexist with nature while still meeting the needs of the people. Gone were the days of exhausting the land and shipping food halfway around the world while millions went hungry. The new system worked for everyone.

As they headed back to the city the next day, Atif was struck by how different everything felt. The city, once a place of stress and hustle, was now calm, yet brimming with energy. The roads were filled with multi-modal transportation systems—electric buses, autonomous cars, bicycles, and trams—working together to make the city more accessible. Commuters, no longer stuck in traffic jams, moved seamlessly from one mode of transport to another. The air was cleaner, the streets quieter, and yet the city had never felt more alive.

Healthcare has undergone a similar transformation. Once a luxury for the few, it was now a basic right for all. The Customer Service Reps—community helpers who had become a cornerstone of the new world—played a crucial role. They provided support, guidance, and care to every person who needed it. No one had to navigate the healthcare system alone.

The AI-driven medical systems ensured that every citizen had access to timely, affordable, and personalized care while the Customer Service Reps were there to provide the human touch.

In this world, work and income have finally been decoupled. People were no longer chained to jobs they despised, working long hours just to make ends meet. Instead, they chose work that brought them joy, fulfillment, and meaning. Most people worked just a few hours a day, spending the rest of their time with family, friends, and their communities. The pressures of modern life had eased, and in their place came a deeper connection to the things that truly mattered.

Sarah, standing beside Atif, observed the city's transformation with pride. "Remember when we first started talking about Peopleism?" she asked. "How impossible it all seemed?"

Atif smiled. "I do. But look at it now. People are working less, living more, and no one's being left behind."

The old economic systems that had once defined the world—capitalism, socialism, communism—were now relics of the past. Peopleism had succeeded where those systems had failed. It created a society where technology and wealth were shared, where no one was left out, and where everyone had the chance to thrive. It was not perfect—nothing ever is—but it was a far cry from the world they had once known.

For Atif, this moment was bittersweet. He thought back to the early days when they were still grappling with the enormity of what they were trying to accomplish. There had been resistance, of course—many had clung to the old ways, fearful of change. But over time, the logic of Peopleism became undeniable. It was not just about economic theory or political ideology—it was about people—real people, living real lives, and making sure that everyone had a place in the future.

Sarah, sensing Atif's reflective mood, placed a hand on his shoulder. "We did it," she said softly.

Atif nodded, his eyes scanning the city before him, then turning back toward the countryside where their journey had begun. "We did it for the people,"

As the sun set on that day, Atif felt a profound sense of peace. The world had changed. They had changed it. And though there were still challenges ahead, he knew, deep down, that they had set humanity on a path toward something better. The age of capitalism was over, but the lessons it had taught them would not be forgotten. Peopleism, born from the trials and tribulations of the past, had ushered in a new era—one of balance, fairness, and above all, hope.

And so, as Atif and Sarah stood together, gazing out at the world they had helped create, they knew that the future was bright, not just for them, but for everyone.

www.ingramcontent.com/pod-product-compliance
Lightning Source LLC
Chambersburg PA
CBHW031141130726
47988CB00006B/2475